EASTERN WISDOM,
MODERN LIFE

T0126050

EASTERN WISDOM, MODERN LIFE

COLLECTED TALKS
1960–1969

ALAN WATTS

NEW WORLD LIBRARY
NOVATO, CALIFORNIA

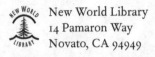 New World Library
14 Pamaron Way
Novato, CA 94949

Copyright © 1994, 1995, 1998, and 2006 by Alan Watts

All rights reserved. This book may not be reproduced in whole or in part, stored in a retrieval system, or transmitted in any form or by any means — electronic, mechanical, or other — without written permission from the publisher, except by a reviewer, who may quote brief passages in a review.

Chapters 4, 8, 10, 13, and 16 appeared earlier in the book *The Culture of Counter-Culture*, copyright © 1998. Chapters 5, 7, 14, and 15 appeared earlier in the book *Myth and Religion*, copyright © 1995. Chapter 12 first appeared in the book *Talking Zen*, copyright © 1994.

Interior design by Tona Pearce Myers

Library of Congress Cataloging-in-Publication Data
Watts, Alan, 1915–1973.
  Eastern wisdom, modern life : collected talks 1960–1969 / Alan Watts.
— 1st ed.
    p.   cm.
Includes bibliographical references.
ISBN 978-1-57731-180-5 (pbk. : alk. paper)
  1. Asia—Religion. 2. Philosophy, Asian. I. Title.
BL1055.W377 2006
294.3—dc22   2006014342

First printing, October 2006
ISBN 978-1-57731-180-5
Printed in Canada

 New World Library is proud to be a Gold Certified Environmentally Responsible Publisher. Publisher certification awarded by Green Press Initiative. www.greenpressinitiative.org

10 9 8 7

CONTENTS

PART THREE: 1965–1967

PART FOUR: 1968–1969

FOREWORD

EASTERN WISDOM, MODERN LIFE draws upon works from a pivotal
decade in the life and works of Alan Watts, a time in which he pio-
neered ideas and ways of knowing that helped shape the cultural
landscape of the 1960s and beyond. A foremost interpreter of Far
Eastern wisdom for the Western world, he explored the frontiers of
human knowledge, a place where perception and inquiry become
the yin and yang of the essential questions "Who Am I?" "What
is the meaning of life?" and "Why are we here?"

A native of England, Alan Watts attended the King's School
near Canterbury Cathedral, and at the age of fourteen he became
fascinated with the philosophies of the Far East. By sixteen he reg-
ularly attended the Buddhist Lodge in London, where he met Zen
scholars Christmas Humphries and D. T. Suzuki. As a speaker and
contributor to the Lodge's journal, *The Middle Way*, he wrote a
series of philosophical commentaries and published his first book
on Eastern thought, *The Spirit of Zen*, at age twenty-one.

In the late thirties he moved to New York, and a few years later he became an Episcopalian priest. In 1942 he moved to Illinois and spent the wartime years as chaplain at Northwestern University.

Then, in 1950, he left the Church, and his life took a turn away from organized religion back toward Eastern ways and expanding horizons. After meeting author and mythologist Joseph Campbell and composer John Cage in New York he headed to California and began teaching at the American Academy of Asian Studies in San Francisco. There his popular lectures spilled over into coffeehouse talks and appearances with the well-known beat writers Gary Snyder, Jack Kerouac, and Allen Ginsberg. In late 1953 he began what would become the longest running series of Sunday morning public radio talks, which continue to this day with programs from the Alan Watts tape archives. In 1957 he published the bestselling *The Way of Zen*, beginning a prolific ten-year period in which he wrote *Nature, Man and Woman*; *Beat Zen, Square Zen and Zen*; *This Is It*; *Psychotherapy East and West*; *The Two Hands of God*; *The Joyous Cosmology*; and *The Book: On the Taboo against Knowing Who You Are*.

By 1960 Watts's radio series *Way Beyond the West* on Berkeley's KPFA had an avid following on the West Coast, and NET television began national broadcasts of the series *Eastern Wisdom in Modern Life*. The first season, recorded in the studios of KQED, a San Francisco television station, focused on the relevance of Buddhism, and the second, on Zen and the arts. The chapters in part 1 of this book were adapted from the opening programs in the second season, including "Buddha and Buddhism," "Mahayana Buddhism," and "The Discipline of Zen." They were intended to introduce the Buddhist approach to the psychology of religion.

The chapters in part 2 were drawn from some of Watts's engaging public lectures between 1963 and 1965. They include talks he gave at major universities, on "Mysticism and Morality," "The Images of Man," "The Relevance of Oriental Philosophy," and

"Religion and Sexuality." In these talks he delivered powerful and pointed critiques of the role of Western religion in modern society and proposed a broader view of the divine to receptive young audiences.

Part 3 is based on seminars and lectures recorded between 1965 and 1967 and includes deeply considered perspectives on "From Time to Eternity," leading into the "Philosophy of Nature," as he called the philosophy of the Tao, or Way. In "Taoist Ways" and "Swimming Headless," one finds a profound appreciation for the course and current of nature, including our own nature as human beings. Part 3 ends with "Zen Bones," a stirring talk on the Zen methods of intellectual liberation and an introduction to the realm of mystical vision.

The fourth and final part picks up where part 3 leaves off, with "Divine Alchemy," a 1968 talk on the use of sacraments specifically and mystical experience generally. Then, in the final three talks, "Democracy in Heaven," "Not What Should Be, but What Is!" and "What Is Reality?" Watts raises and answers the question "Where do we go from here?" providing suggestions for living "with the Tao" in contemporary society.

Although the following selections are only a handful of the many talks Alan Watts gave in the sixties, they have been selected to represent the whole, and to present the highlights of a career that reflected the philosophical openness of the sixties and paved the way for the flood of interest in the traditions of the Far East that followed.

— Mark Watts

PART ONE

1960

CHAPTER ONE

BUDDHA AND BUDDHISM

IN THIS SERIES OF ARTICLES on Eastern wisdom and modern life, I'm going to be exploring Buddhism and Zen, Zen being a particular form of Buddhism which flourishes in Japan and China.

You may wonder why I am particularly interested in investigating Buddhism as distinct from other forms of Asian philosophy and religion. The reason is that Buddhism is a method of liberation which has emerged as a way of life in Asia, but which is not so closely tied to the different cultures of Asia as such other philosophies or religions as Hinduism or Confucianism or Shinto. Shinto, for example, is the national cult of Japan, and it would be impossible, really, for Shinto to migrate to any other people than the Japanese. In the same way, Confucianism is intimately bound up with Chinese culture. And also Hinduism is tied to the particular culture and social order of India. Although it began in India, Buddhism has migrated to all parts of Asia and has adapted itself to all kinds of different cultures. And so, in this way you might say Buddhism is an intercultural or even international way of life, and therefore of all the forms of Asian philosophy it is probably of most interest to the West.

However there are certain difficulties in trying to introduce the idea of Buddhism at all because it's ordinarily looked upon as a form of religion. When, for example, we look at studies of comparative religions, Buddhism is grouped together with Christianity, with Judaism, with Islam, with Zoroastrianism, and with Hinduism — as if all these were things of the same kind. But I think if we use the one word *religion* to designate things so astonishingly different as Christianity and Judaism, on the one hand, and Buddhism, on the other, we make the word have such a wide meaning that it really means nothing at all. Now I don't want to lay down the law as to what religion is, but I think I would make myself more intelligible if I let you know the way I understand the word. And I think it's simplest if we confine the word *religion* to such phenomena as Christianity, or Judaism, or Islam. And then we'll have to find another term for things so different as Buddhism.

What is the difference? The word religion comes from the Latin *religare* – to bind — and thus a religion is the following of a rule of life that is believed to be divinely revealed. There is, in other words, a body of doctrine we call the creed, and this is revealed doctrine, which the human being is supposed to believe. Then there is the revealed way of life — the code — the expression of the will of God in terms of law or, as in Christianity, in terms of the personality of Christ. And then, finally, in religion there is the cult; that is to say the worship of God, of the ultimate reality who has revealed Himself in the form of the religion.

Now Buddhism has neither creed, code, nor cult. There is nothing that is binding upon the Buddhist, nothing they are supposed to believe in. There is no authoritative code, and there are no positive doctrines that the believer has to ascend to. It's true that

Buddhists do observe certain precepts of moral and ethical behavior, however they don't regard the observation of them as following a divine will. It's simply a pledge you take to yourself. And, furthermore, Buddhism has no particular cult. That is to say, there are no specific sacraments or forms of worship that are binding upon all Buddhists. You might then say that Buddhism is a form of philosophy, but again this would not be quite correct because what we understand by philosophy in the West is the elaboration of certain ideas, certain theories about the nature of the universe, the nature of man or the nature of knowledge. And Buddhism is not particularly concerned with elaborating ideas.

The nearest thing in our culture to Buddhism, although it isn't exactly the same, is probably psychotherapy. And the reason is that what constitutes the essence of Buddhism is not beliefs, not ideas, not even practices, but a way of experiencing. I could almost call it a way of feeling. Now in psychotherapy, if a person goes to a psychotherapist because they feel miserable, are depressed, anxious, or profoundly worried, the object of the psychotherapist's practice is to change the person's state of consciousness, to change their state of mind. And, in this respect, it is something like Buddhism because Buddhism envisages a transformation, a very radical transformation, of the way in which ordinary people feel themselves and the surrounding world. And so, in this sense, I have coined for Buddhism a special term to contrast it with a religion. I would call it a "way of liberation," a way of liberation from the ordinary way in which most civilized and probably many primitive people feel themselves and the world. That is to say, for example, the feeling that I am a lonely, separate, transient individual locked up inside my skin, and therefore different from, even hostile to and alienated from, everything else.

Now, of course, if I mention the word *Buddha*, I suppose to many people's minds it refers to the picture of an idol. But the image of a Buddha is a figure of a man, not of a god. Specifically it is a figure of an Indian prince who lived around 560 B.C., and his name was Gautama Siddhartha. This man is called the Buddha, but that's not his proper name. It is a title and it means, approximately, "the man who woke up." Buddha refers to the awakened one, and in saying that Buddhism is something like psychotherapy, it might be correct to say that Gautama, the Buddha, was the world's first great psychotherapist. And it is interesting that the way in which he formulated his method was patterned upon a doctor's prescription. He expressed his treatment in a form called the Four Noble Truths and I'm going to go through these four truths, which are named in the ancient Indian language of Sanskrit. They follow the doctor's method of diagnosing and prescribing, because the first thing a doctor is asked, when he's summoned to the bed of a sick man, is to diagnose what it is he suffers from. And so the first of the Buddha's noble truths is the name of the disease from which human beings suffer, and in Sanskrit that is *duhkha*, which means something approximately like anguish, or suffering in a special sense. The cause of the disease he called *trishna*, and the word *trishna*, which is related to our word *thirst*, means clutching or grasping, and it is often translated "desire." The third thing the doctor is asked is whether the disease can be cured, and if so what the cure might be, and to this he responds in Sanskrit *nirvana*, and that means "release." Finally, having stated the cure, he gives the prescription for the cure and here we have the Sanskrit word *marga*. Marga means "path" and it designates the Noble Eightfold Path, the steps to following the Buddhist way of life.

So let's go back to the meaning of each one of these words, and we go back, first of all, to duhkha, the disease from which human beings are suffering according to the Buddha's method.

Now sometimes this word is given just the very general meaning of suffering, but I think it should be given a more specific sense, and I would call it anguish or chronic frustration as a result of trying to do things that are inherently impossible, and that are inherently contradictory. If you try to draw a square circle, you can try to the end of time but you'll never do it because it's a contradiction. And in the same way, there are certain things which human beings are doing which are contradictory and which get them into a state of chronic anguish.

Now in Buddha's method duhkha stems from another factor which is sort of intermediate between suffering, or anguish, and its cause. And he said that clutching, which is the basis of our anguish, is ultimately dependent upon a kind of unconsciousness or ignorance, which in Sanskrit is called *avidya*, literally "not knowing," thus ignorance. And it is really a way of seeing the world in an unrelated way, and thinking of it as consisting simply of so many things, like a rock, a foot, a plant, a man, when, actually, the world is not composed of bits and pieces. Everything that exists exists only in relation to other things. In other words, an egg, for example, looks very separate. It looks like a very definite, particular thing. But you don't find eggs without chickens. And you don't find chickens without the sort of environment in which chickens can live. Likewise, in a similar fashion you don't find fingers lying around without a hand. Although we think of the fingers as separate, they are related to the hand; the hand, in turn, to the arm; the arm to the body; and the body to its whole environment of earth and sky, sunlight and air.

And so, if we think of the world as being made up of separate things rather than related things, we start trying to deal with things as if they were separate. That is to say, take for example pleasure and pain. We say pleasure is distinctly separate from pain. I want pleasure, but I don't want pain. I would like to have pleasure without pain. And so we set our lives to this task. But actually this is as contradictory as trying to have up without down. Supposing we try to arrange everything around here so that everything was up and there was nothing down, or so that we had all fronts but no backs. We would simply cease to exist. And so, in the same way, to try to wrest or separate pleasure from pain would bring about a state of mind in which we cease to know what pleasure was. There would be no contrast to pleasure and it would become simply boring. And so, in this way, we orient our lives towards impossible ideals and as a result run into frustration.

Another source of frustration arises when we do not see that the world in which we live is fundamentally impermanent. One of the cardinal features of the Buddha's teaching is that all life, however solid it may seem to be, and all things, however separate they may seem to be, are in a state of flux. That is to say that the world we live in doesn't consist so much of things or entities as it consists of process. Everything is in a constant state of flowing pattern. By way of illustration you might say that it's something like the flowing pattern you see when you look at smoke: a dancing, constantly changing arabesque of pattern; flowing, flowing, all the time. Or that the substance of life is something like water, which I can hold in my hand so long as I cup it gently, but if I clutch at the water, I immediately lose it.

And so, in this way, through our failure to see that everything is alive because it flows, we try to possess it, and this is trishna, or grasping. In other words we try to hold on as tight as we can to what we love: to hold on to our own lives, to hold on to the lives of people we cherish. In exactly the same way a mother, who's very fond of a child who's growing up and still wants to keep that baby, and smothers with love that little kid which she adores so much, and is anxious lest the child while growing up should run into mistakes. So she clings to the child, and she refuses to let the child have the full play of responsibility and risk. But this is no different than refusing to let an egg hatch. All that happens is that the egg will get addled inside its shell if it isn't allowed to grow into the chick, to break free, to change. Or, in the same way, you might love the sound of running water that you hear in a stream passing through somebody's garden. And you think, "Oh yes, I'd love to have that water in my own garden." And you arrive there with a bucket, and you pick the water up, and you take it away. But having caught the water in the bucket, it's dead; it's no longer living running water.

So we are constantly frustrated by grasping and strangling a world that is essentially a changing pattern. Now of course in our ordinary common sense we do think of the world as pattern, but as patterns of something. In other words, we think that underneath all form, all shape, all pattern, there is some solid stuff that we might call substance, and this is based on thinking that the world is made in the same way as a potter makes pots out of clay. And therefore we think it quite natural to ask: "What are stars made of?" "What are mountains made of?" "What are trees made of?" We assume that they were constructed and that they were constructed out of something, like a carpenter makes tables out of wood or the potter makes pots out of clay. But really this is an unnecessary notion because the stuff underlying things, when we inquire into it in our own modern science, turns out to be evermore complex and subtle patterns. If you take something that looks very solid and metallic, like a coin, it has a good hard, dense surface. But look at this same dense, polished surface under an electron microscope and what you see is pattern. Or look at it more deeply, from the standpoint of the nuclear physicist, and it's simply dancing orbits of energy. So, if we have a picture of the world in which we think that beneath all changing forms there lies solid stuff, then in the same way we come to have an idea of ourselves as a sort of stuff underlying the changing form of our actions. We think of ourselves as doers behind thoughts and words and deed, as experiencers behind experience.

But if we were to realize that we are, as it were, all action, all deed — the doer vanishes, and with it vanishes this sense of man as something separate, something cut off, walled away from the rest of the world by his skin. When that realization comes about; when, in other words, our own separateness disappears, we have what the Buddha called nirvana — release, or the cure. But nirvana is a terribly misunderstood word. A lot of people, when they hear the word *nirvana*, think, "Well, it's sort of a state of being, a place vaguely, dreamily blissful." It's like you might feel on a Sunday afternoon after an enormous dinner. Or they think it means annihilation. Strictly speaking, though, this word in Sanskrit means simply to "blow out," that is, blow out in the sense of "wheeeeew," to breathe a sigh of relief. And this word was chosen because breath is one of the fundamental symbols of life. The word *spirit* is, originally, one's breath, and if I were to think: "I've got to have breath, I need my breath, my breath is my life and therefore I hold my breath," then, like keeping water in the bucket, I begin to lose my breath and turn purple in the face. So instead I have to let go, breathe out, and lose my breath in order to have breath. So you might say that the whole idea of clinging is put in the metaphor of trying to hold on to one's breath, trying to hold on to one's life, refusing to let one's self go. But when that is seen to be impossible, just as it's impossible to have pleasure all the time and no pain, then one lives what you might call "the blown out life" — the life of nirvana.

And finally the Buddha describes marga, the path that leads to awakening. I'm not going to go into all the details, the eight steps, or the eight folds of the Buddha's marga, or path, instead for now I'll just touch on the spirit of it. Buddha called the path the Middle Way and so you might say this is the path of the middle road. This is often misunderstood as a way of what you might call compromise. In Buddha's time there were many people in India seeking liberation from suffering by extreme forms of asceticism and self-mortification. And naturally on the other hand there were other people trying to escape from suffering by intense pleasure seeking, as we can see today. But Buddha said both these roads were ignoble, both the road of self-mortification, lying on beds of nails and the like, and the road of pleasure seeking, or hedonism.

But the Middle Way does not quite mean a compromise between these two extremes.

It has a somewhat more profound sense than that, and I think the easiest way of understanding what the Buddha meant by "the middle way" would be to call it "the balanced life" — avoiding falling into one extreme or to another extreme. When you ride a bicycle, you do something that is very much like following the Middle Way, because to stay upright as you go along you balance to avoid falling to either side. But the curious thing about riding a bicycle, which is so difficult for beginners to understand, is that when you start falling, say to the right, you have to turn the handlebars and the wheel to the right, to the direction in which you're falling. And as a result of this, surprisingly enough, you come upright. One would ordinarily think, perhaps, that if you start falling to the right you should turn your wheel to the left, but if you do that you'll collapse.

Now if we apply this analogy of riding the bicycle to Buddhism it sounds something like this: supposing we are falling into fear and we resist fear. Then, what happens? If we resist fear, we begin to be afraid of fear and this leads to what we call worry or anxiety. After all, worry is being afraid of being afraid. And then being afraid because I'm afraid I'm afraid, so it goes on in a vicious circle indefinitely. Now you might say, to use a popular expression, the Middle Way is to "get with it," and "be yourself." Just as the cyclist goes with the direction of his fall and so comes upright again, so the person who suffers from worry, or some interior feeling or mood that bothers them, is advised to "get with it." Now this has a curious effect: it neutralizes the feeling from which you're suffering. This is like what happens if you take a child and put the child in the middle of the room and you say, "Now dear, play." The child is embarrassed. When you are worried, and you say to yourself, "All right, worry. Get with that worry," it neutralizes the worry because you are not worrying about not worrying anymore.

And as a result of this flip, this acceptance of what goes on anyway, the constant conflict which people ordinarily feel between themselves and their feelings, between themselves and their experiences, begins to disappear because they "get with" what they are experiencing, and they don't resist it anymore. And, just as it is a surprise to the beginner on the bicycle to regain control over his machine when he turns in the direction of his fall, so it is an enormous surprise to human beings to find that when they accept themselves instead of fighting themselves they're in much better control of themselves. Somebody who is divided against themselves is like a person trying to ride off in two directions at once, and lives in contradiction. So the ultimate experience of Buddhism is that when we come together with ourselves again, as a result of coming together with ourselves we find that we are together with everything. We are not separate, cutoff beings, but that this whole universe is our self.

CHAPTER TWO

MAHAYANA BUDDHISM

IN THE LAST CHAPTER I introduced the teaching of the Buddha, a man who lived in India about six hundred years before Christ, and in this chapter I'll go further into the original doctrine of Buddhism called Mahayana Buddhism. *Maha* means great in Sanskrit, and *yana* means something like vehicle, or a conveyance. Mahayana Buddhism is found traditionally in the northern part of Asia, primarily in Tibet, China, Mongolia, and Japan. It is often contrasted with another form of Buddhism that is properly called Theravada, which means the Way of the Elders or the Doctrine of the Elders, but is impolitely known as Hinayana, or the little vehicle. This form of Buddhism is found in the south of Asia, in Ceylon, Burma, Thailand, and Cambodia.

The Mahayana school developed in India between approximately 100 B.C. and A.D. 400, which encompasses various periods of its germination, and it is a very profound philosophical elaboration of the Buddha's original teachings. By drawing out certain things that were implicit in those teachings, if not actually stated, it works on the principle that the original teachings are something like a seed, which — if it has any vitality in it at all — grows into a tree. However sometimes the tree doesn't look very much like its seed, although the tree was of course implicit in the seed from the beginning. This form of the traditional teachings of the Buddha spread from northern India to China, and Tibet, and it is from Chinese, Indian, and Tibetan sources that we have some of the most accessible Buddhist texts.

Now once upon a time there was an old Chinese Buddhist master called Lin Chi, and he used to tell his disciples that he felt his duty toward them was to beat the ghosts out of them. And as I pointed out to you before, Buddhism is in a certain sense an awakening: a waking up, as it were, from a bad dream, and in this sense ghosts are something like a bad dream. They are, as it were, certain fixed ideas or habits of thought which, to use a slang phrase, "hang up" the human mind and confuse us.

One of these habits, which is very carefully investigated in Mahayana Buddhism, is the idea that this world is not really what we would call substantial. There is a theory in Mahayana Buddhism that is called the doctrine of "mind only." It isn't quite like Western ideas that we sometimes call subjective idealism, in other words the idea that the whole world is something that exists only in your own mind, and there isn't any outside world "out there" at all. In the Buddha's original teaching is the idea that the whole of our world of experience is the perception of pure pattern, which is as it were formation or process, without any substantiality in it at all. What we experience is a pattern of form constantly rippling and changing and shifting, and always flowing from one thing to another. So then try and conceive of all the things of the world as form, and nothing but form, and as having no stuff underneath the constantly shifting shapes that change before your eyes. Of course this is a difficult idea for us to imagine because it's so contrary to our ordinary common sense.

As I explained in the last chapter, we tend to think of our world by analogy with the potter's craft, as a material construct. Just as a potter makes pots out of clay, so we think of all the various things in the world — the mountains, the stars, the trees, people, and so on — as being made out of some stuff. But as we know from modern science, and as the old Buddhist philosophers knew in earlier times, we can perfectly well give an account of this world, describe it, and talk about it in terms of form alone without ever having to introduce the concept of stuff. And that's only a difficult idea for us to understand because we have fixed habits of thought that make it seem strange to us when we try to clarify it.

Now this involves another idea that is common to all schools of Buddhism, which again, for the same reason, is difficult for us to understand, and this is called in Sanskrit the doctrine of *anatman* — which means non-ego. This is to say that the feeling that we have of being "I," a thinker behind thought, an experiencer behind experience, a feeler behind our feelings, and a senser behind our sensations, is understood by all schools of Buddhist thought to be an illusion. But this immediately surprises us because it seems to be one of the most common sense feelings we could have. Not simply that I am I, in the sense that I am my whole physical organism and body, but also the feeling that there is some kind of permanent entity or center of consciousness inside the body receiving all its experiences and being the main director of its actions. This entity is sitting in the body like a chauffeur inside an automobile, as if we had some sort of little man inside our heads. And so it does seem fundamental, a commonsense idea, that we, as ego, as I myself, as the knower, the little man inside the head, am a sort of screen upon which life is constantly writing a pattern. And we develop from this the fear that the writing of life upon the screen may wear the pattern out in the same way, for example, as if I were to write on a sheet of paper, and begin to trace patterns on it, eventually the page will fill up and turn black, and we have as it were the impression that the constant motion of life is wearing out the conscious knower — the ego — and therefore we develop a kind of resistance to experience.

But now I think we ought to ask the question, Is this really true?

Is experience something that happens to us, something that we "have"?

Or would it be more accurate to say that there is simply a process of experiencing? Again, the Buddhist philosophers of ancient India had realized something, which we can perhaps see even more clearly as a result of our own scientific investigations of just what perception is in terms of neurology. This is not to say that our consciousness or our minds are nothing but a tangle of nerves, because that sounds like a kind of materialism. We can think of our nervous system simply as a pattern, because the important point to realize first is that all that we see in terms of an outside world — color, texture, shape, and so on — is going on inside our heads. For example when we touch something, and feel that it's hard, what we're actually experiencing is not so much the outside thing, although it's true the stimulus is coming from the outside world to our body. But what we actually feel and experience as hardness is a particular activity or process going on inside our nervous system. So we could say all of our experience of the external world is felt directly only as an experience of the nervous system. And even that, in a way, is not quite correct because when I say "an experience of the nervous system," or that "what we are experiencing is a state of our nervous system," this still isn't a simple enough way of talking about it, because it sounds again as if there were, behind the nervous system itself, a separate "experiencer."

So what we have to try and get clear is that our sensations are processes in the nervous system, and that those processes are us. The self is the actual process of sensation — there isn't a senser behind sensation. When we have a sensation we don't have it, we are it. And so it helps, then, if first of all we could think of the nervous system as being a pure pattern, something like the patterns of a branching tree. Now our nervous system has in it a peculiar capacity, which is illustrated by the tree in that if you look closely you'll notice that the patterns of each leaf reflect an evolution of the pattern of the entire tree. The preceding pattern is represented in the following one, which as it were adapts the former state of the pattern. In other words, the former state of this pattern that we call a leaf was also a tree, and if we turn the whole thing upside down and look at the roots, we will see the same pattern, the same intelligence, reflected in the roots. As we shift from one level of magnification to another, the patterns change, but what we find inside is a subpattern, or subsection of the main pattern, which represents the previous one, and of course it represents the first one as well. And so when we look at the overall structure we find that each level of pattern has its own specialized use of the form, but there is an overall adaptive form that resembles every other form in the tree.

The ability of a pattern to contain elements that represent its former states is what we call memory. In engineering language we would call it feedback, because feedback is the system whereby any system of energy is enabled to record the results of its own action so that based upon that record it can adapt, and as it were make plans for the future. It can, in other words, correct its action. So because human beings have memory, the capacity of the pattern of the nervous system to record its former states, the human being can make predictions about the future and in general control its activity.

But from this extraordinarily marvelous ability there arises a certain confusing byproduct. And that is this feeling that there is a constant entity, like the screen of a television set. In other words, because a certain element of permanence runs through these changing patterns, this permanent behavior of the pattern, or permanently repeating behavior of the pattern, gives the impression of some substantial mind stuff or mind entity underlying the pattern and upon which the pattern in recorded. It's the same sort of illusion that arises when, for example, I take a flashlight and rotate it in the dark, and you see a continuous circle of light. It appears that the light leaves a track behind it because the moving light leaves a memory upon the retina of the eye, and that is what gives us the illusion of seeing a constant circle of light.

And so a similar illusion arises from the repetitive pattern of the nervous system, and gives us the impression that there is this constant thing, the experiencer, who lasts, and endures like a substance from the past, through the present, and into the future. But at the same time, it has to protect itself against being worn out by experience, and so gradually we come to develop within ourselves a resistance to what we are experiencing. And this comes about not only because we are afraid of being worn out, but also because the problem of control constantly arises. We become anxious as to whether our predictions are going to work out, and therefore we tend to become overly cautious, questioning whether our acts are exactly right or exactly wrong, or whether our thoughts about them are exactly right or exactly wrong.

As a result of this anxiety and expectation our resistance to experience builds up. But what this does is to make the whole system, the whole flowing of the pattern, operate less efficiently because it becomes "sticky." Supposing when I write I resist my own action of writing. And instead of writing what I am thinking and feeling I begin to question whether I am thinking about the subject correctly. This reflection is good from time to time, but when it becomes constant it interrupts the flow of ideas and feelings. If this loop is amplified it shakes up the system, and in very much the same way we begin to develop the kind of chronic shakiness, which we call anxiety, when we start resisting our own process of feeling too much. And as a result of that resistance we get not only chronic anxiety, but also a chronic feeling of frustration.

Then we begin to feel as though something's got to be done about this too. But what does that lead to? It just leads to more of the same kind of thing. In other words, if we identify ourselves with this permanent and purely illusory ego substance, that really isn't there, we're identifying ourselves with something abstract. We get from this a kind of hunger which is not physical but psychic. And from that we develop a greed for events — for more and more experience; for more and more life. And yet at the same time we know that the more we experience and the longer and harder we live, the more it's going to wear us out. And so this kind of resistance to life leads to further resistance and becomes a vicious circle, which in Buddhist philosophy is called *samsara*, the round of existence. And although samsara is represented in popular Buddhist philosophy as a process of the individual being reincarnated into this world again and again and again and again, so long as one has attraction for it, the real meaning of the circle of reincarnation, of the going round and round, is precisely the same vicious circle which arises through a resistance to life, which builds up into greater and greater frustration.

Now we can demonstrate this in rather an interesting way

because just as this is an attempt to split the human mind apart and turn it back on itself, so we could create a situation in the television circuit whereby we turn the television circuit back onto itself by pointing the camera at the monitor. And the kind of infinite regression of images that we get when we do this is exactly what happens to our minds when we develop excessive self-consciousness, which is to say, an excessive sensation of difference between the experiencer and the experience. And when we try to make the one latch on to the other completely and control it — when the experiencer resists experience — what really happens is that the whole pattern of our consciousness, of our nervous system, gets sticky and begins to jangle. And under such conditions, when for example we are worrying about worrying and worrying about worrying about worrying, life becomes an intolerable burden.

And so then it was for this reason that the original appeal of Buddhism to the human mind was that it offered a way of deliverance from the vicious circle of life. But here we see an important point that is fundamental to the thinking of Mahayana Buddhism — that trying to get out is still working on the assumption that there is a real experiencer to be extracted from experience. But what we've just discovered is that that is the illusion: there is no experiencer to be extracted, no one who can escape from experience. There is simply experiencing, just the moving pattern, and in the symbolism of Mahayana Buddhism the person who is no longer seeking an escape from life, but has realized that it isn't something to be escaped from, is called in Sanskrit a *bodhisattva*. And one of the most famous of the bodhisattvas was Kuan-yin, the bodhisattva of mercy. Bodhisattvas are thought of as ones who have come back into the world of everyday events, and are there to live in it fully and to help all other beings to be delivered.

In other words, the ideal of Mahayana Buddhist wisdom is not a detached and aloof sort of sage who shuns life, but one who loves life and therefore gets thoroughly involved in it. The bodhisattva is thought of as one who is not afraid to assume any form symbolically, and therefore represents the whole attitude of overcoming life not by escaping from it, but by accepting it completely and profoundly, through and through. There is no one separate from it to do the accepting, and so there is an ancient Buddhist verse which says:

> Suffering alone exists, no one who suffers.
> Deeds alone exist, but no doer;
> The path there is, but no one who treads it.
> Nirvana exists, but no one who attains it.

So you may ask then, Well what is this all about? If there are deeds but no doer, experiencing but no experiencer, then what is reality? What is life? After all, we always thought we knew what pattern was by contrast with stuff, substance with form, but now if the contrast has disappeared, we are left with the deed alone, but no agent; the form alone, but no stuff. So what are we left with? This is what Buddhist philosophy calls *shunyata* — the empty void. It is Void, not because there's nothing there, but because our mind has no idea of it.

CHAPTER THREE

THE DISCIPLINE OF ZEN

IN THE FOLLOWING SESSIONS we will look into the ways of early Chinese Zen masters, because it was through the influence of Chinese life that Mahayana Buddhism took on a particular flavor and style of expression that became Ch'an Buddhism in China, and Zen in Japan. When one looks at a Zen garden in Japan, you might not believe it, but it is a form of religious art: no images, no symbols; just natural rock and raked sand — a form of art which is in a way extraordinarily unlike anything else in the world. This unique expression of natural beauty and simplicity is just as much a manifestation of spirituality as any of the religious art of the West; as the Christs and the Madonnas of Giotto or Fra Angelico. But you will notice that there's no image in Zen art, and no attempt to represent anything but what it is — just rock and sand. And in this way these gardens incomparably express that astonishing form of Buddhism known as Zen.

The earthy style of pottery bowl from which Zen monks drink tea is executed in the same spirit. It's very simple, rather rugged and unpretentious. The glaze doesn't even cover the whole form, so you see it's quite obviously made of clay. And yet tea bowls are icons, just as much spiritual objects as a cross or a chalice. And they are icons just because they are simple tea bowls. And you might not think there is very much in the way of technique in these bowls, just a rough old bowl looking like rocks and sand from the garden. But you would be mistaken. You can see examples of very obvious technical dexterity throughout Japanese Buddhist art in the sixteenth century, and it's intention is no more than to show us wild landscapes and natural habitats in which one becomes again a part of nature.

However in the Western world we're accustomed very much to thinking of spiritual things as being set apart and distinctly separate from everyday life. We think of the spiritual as being out of this world, or otherworldly, and not of the natural world. Therefore in the West all those art forms, which deal with spiritual things, deal with symbols of the divine, which attempt to transcend everyday materiality. But in the art of Chinese and Japanese Zen Buddhism we see a concentration on everyday life. And even when the great sages of Buddhism are depicted, they're depicted in a secular style, just like very ordinary people, and often like the lowest class of people; wandering idiots and tramps.

And the meaning of this is that their attitude about the relationship of soul to body, or mind to matter, is entirely different from ours. In fact, they don't really consider the spiritual life in those kinds of categories at all. Because we divide the soul from body, and separate spirit from matter, God is experienced as separate from the world. And therefore, as we confront this material world, identifying ourselves with a kind of inner soul, we feel we have a problem. We feel that life must either be conquered, or somehow we must get out of it. But either way we always feel distinct from it. We think of man not so much as part of the natural material world, but man as separate from it, dominating it, and trying to master it.

But the Zen art forms found in Japan and China express quite a different point of view, a point of view for which the material, ordinary, everyday world is not a problem to be solved. That would really be rather a relief, wouldn't it, if we could feel it that way? But as you remember in the last session, I've been talking about Buddhism, and as we begin to explore the native Chinese philosophy of Taoism you will see that they have one essential point in common, and that is the view of life as a flowing process in which humankind, and the mind and the consciousness of human beings, is inextricably involved. But this isn't as though there is a fixed kind of screen, a canvas of consciousness over which this process of experience flows, and leaves a record. It is that human consciousness itself is part of the flowing process and therefore, for this reason, man, and the mind of man, is not a separate entity observing the process from outside, but it is involved with all of it.

And therefore any fundamental conflict between the mind of man and the flow of life is, in terms of this philosophy, unreal, an illusion — something that is imagined. And I tried to explain in the last chapter, this illusion arises because of the fact that the human memory is a part of this flowing pattern, and because it has the ability to represent former states of the pattern. And that memory gives the illusion of a certain permanence to the behavior of the pattern, but that permanence is not the same thing as a kind of soul substance, or a mind substance separate from the pattern upon which the record is written.

Now in China, about A.D. 400 and a little thereafter, there was a great effort undertaken to translate Indian Buddhist ideas into Chinese. And in finding suitable ideas in Chinese thought and in

Chinese language to translate Buddhism so as to be intelligible to the Chinese mind, the philosophy that came most naturally to hand was Taoism. So, at this time in Chinese history, Buddhism and Taoism flowed together, and the product of their coming together, being very much akin to each other, was a form of Buddhism peculiarly Chinese, in that it's highly definite in all its images. The teachings of Indian Buddhism, which were recorded in Sanskrit, tended to be speculative, abstract, philosophical, and metaphysical. But the Chinese language is an extremely practical and concrete language, being originally based, as you know, on pictures rather than on sounds. And therefore, when Buddhism came into China, and was translated into Chinese, the feeling it assumed was very down-to-earth, and took on the form that is known most commonly by its Japanese name, Zen.

Now Zen is the way of realizing, or making real, the theory of Buddhism so that it's not just something that you know about in your head, but something that you feel in your bones. And as a way of realization Zen Buddhism is the Japanese word for the Chinese Ch'an, which, in turn, is the Chinese pronunciation of the Indian Sanskrit word *dhyana*. The problem that I have here is to try and give an English equivalent of this term. Sometimes this word dhyana in Sanskrit is translated "meditation." But this is misleading. Perhaps the best word I could give as an equivalent for what Zen means is concentration, although this is rather different from what we understand by concentration in the ordinary sense; that is to say, an intense mental effort to hold one's mind upon a single point.

I would call it concentration in the sense of being free from distraction, a sense of total presence of mind; of being, shall we say, thoroughly all there. Most of us in our thinking are wandering from this to that to the other thing, and are constantly distracted. And Zen is the opposite of that. It's being completely here, fully in the present. And you know when you're completely concentrated, you're not really aware of your own existence. It's rather the same as the sense of sight. If you see your eyes, that is to say if you see spots in front of your eyes, or something on the lens of the eye, then you're not seeing properly. To the degree to which you're seeing properly, you're unaware of your eyes. In the same way, if your clothes fit well, you're unaware of them on your body. And if you're completely concentrated on what you're doing, you're unaware of yourself.

And this unawareness of self is called in Chinese *wu shin*, which we will talk about more in the following sessions, but it means literally, "no mind," but not "no mind" in the sense of having no sense and being stupid. The second word, *shin* in Chinese, is approximately what we would mean by the ego, the "I-sense" that I described before: the sense of being somebody standing apart, observing your sensations, thinking your thoughts and feeling your feelings. So wu shin, or in Japanese *mu shin*, means, perhaps more accurately, "no self." This is the state in which one is completely involved in, completely absorbed in, what one's doing — in a state of complete presence of mind or complete concentration.

Now, according to legend, Zen was brought from India to China probably around A.D. 500 by a person called Bodhidharma, who is always depicted as a rather fierce looking fellow with a bushy beard and big, wide awake eyes. He is thoroughly alert, and although he may be a legendary character, there's rather an important story about his interview with his first and only disciple, a Chinese monk by the name of Hui-k'o. Hui-k'o came to Bodhidharma with the usual troubles that afflict us all, and he said, "Master, I have no peace of mind," and the word he used was shin. "Please pacify my mind." In other words he was a man suffering from the perennial human problem of inner anxiety, the sense of a kind of psychological wobble that is going around here and grinding in most of us much of the time. And he wanted it set at peace. So he said, "Master, I have no peace of mind. Please pacify my mind." And so Bodhidharma, who was a gruff old boy, said, "Bring your mind out here before me. I'll pacify it." And Hui-k'o said, "But when I look for my mind, I can't find it." And Bodhidharma said, "There, it's pacified." Immediately, Hui-k'o had an insight into the meaning of Zen, because when he tried to realize his mind as something actual and concrete and physical, he couldn't find it. It just wasn't there.

The man who is even more responsible for the development of Chinese Zen than Bodhidharma is known as Hui-neng, who lived in the eighth century, and died in 713. Before he was a great Buddhist master, he was a bamboo cutter and when you see pictures of him he is drawn in a very rough, peasantlike, earthy kind of way, which was the style many of those artists favored. As a boy this man somehow came quite naturally to an understanding of Buddhism and sought out one of the greatest masters of his time, who it is said presided over a monastery of more than a thousand Buddhist monks.

However most of those monks seemed to be going about the whole problem of attaining peace of mind in a way that was quite contrary to the real spirit of Buddhism and of Zen. That is to say, they were trying to attain an inner peace by suppressing their thoughts. And you may think, if you've seen figures of the Buddha sitting quietly in meditation with his eyes closed, that that's what he's doing. He's just sitting with his mind blank so that nothing at all bothers him, which happens to be a lot of people's idea of nirvana. But Hui-neng pointed out to those monks that if silence was all that wisdom consists of, and that's what Buddhism is all about, then a piece of rock would be the same as an enlightened Buddha, because a piece of rock has no mind at all. It's not thinking any thoughts, and it's just as dead as can be. And therefore, if your way to peace of mind is to suppress all thoughts, suppress all emotions, suppress all sensations and feelings, then you become a stone Buddha instead of a living Buddha.

It is not enough to be interiorly silent, and we all know that to be completely present in mind, to be fully in what we are doing, is to remain very much alive. It makes for not only inner peace but efficiency in all of our deeds and in everyday life. And therefore we often say to people, "Well, just take things one at a time. It's so easy to do things that way." "Keep your mind on your job." "Concentrate." But the difficulty with this is that if our concentration in our work is a constant effort, is something, in other words, we have to exercise ourselves to do all the time, then as soon as our strength flags a little, then off it goes and we lose it. That's the same as saying, "Oh you ought to concentrate." Or, "You ought to be fully aware of what's going on around you." And you, as it were, force your mind to focus on it. It's a forced action.

Hui-neng learned that you don't achieve this by force, but you achieve it by insight. While one school of thought is trying to pacify the mind by ironing out the thoughts, the other is leaving it alone. And as a matter of fact trying to calm your mind is about as effective a way of getting a calm mind as trying to smooth rough water with a flat iron. The other way is to realize that there is as it were no ego; no stuff to whom thoughts happen, no one to whom experience happens. And through that insight, the idea of the constant entity called the ego, to whom life happens, and for whom life is a problem, is seen to be unreal. There is no past. There is always only a present. As one Buddhist master put it, "We don't say that spring becomes summer. We say there is spring and then there is summer." In other words, we don't have to try to live in the present. We have to understand that only the present is real. There is no past. There is no future.

Look at the practical wisdom of this in a great undertaking, like climbing a mountain. You've got a long task ahead of you and if you keep looking up at the top, you'll feel wearier and wearier, and every step becomes like lead. Or, if you're a housewife washing dishes, and you've got a great pile of dishes by the sink, and you begin to think as you wash through them that you've washed dishes for years, and you're probably going to have to wash dishes for the rest of your life, then in your mind's eye you see this prodigious pile of dishes piling up as high as the Empire State Building. This has been your drudgery in the kitchen all your life, and will be for all the years to come, and you are appalled and oppressed. But dispelling this dread isn't a matter of trying to forget about washing dishes, it is realizing that in actual fact you only have one dish to wash, ever: this one; only one step to take, ever: this one. And that is Zen.

That is concentration at its best. So then, our problem is that we feel inside us a constant struggle, or fight, with time — the tension between the present, on the one hand, and the past and the future on the other. We may feel it as a kind of uneasy feeling in the stomach. Or we may feel it as tension in our head, somewhere behind the eyes. There arises a constant sense of having to struggle to beat time, to keep up with it, and actually this doesn't do anything for us at all. It doesn't enable us to perform our work or conduct our business any better. All it does is put us in a conflict with ourselves, which holds everything up.

And therefore, the first thing that is necessary to learn in the study of Zen is to be quiet, but not to be like a log, with nothing in mind. Instead simply to be all here, and that's why in Zen enormous importance is attached to knowing how to sit. Just sit, and you'll see often Zen monks in a position with their knees folded, sitting quietly. And you may think that's a great waste of time, to sit just like this, maybe for a long time, maybe for an hour, maybe for two hours, sometimes for a whole day. But the point is that a person who can't really sit as if there were nothing else to do also won't be able to act because he'll never be completely all here.

So when you learn to sit, and just sit and become completely present, you naturally become completely quiet, with none of that jazz going on inside. Once you are fully present, and that which we call ourselves falls silent, you can move. One of the great Zen masters, when asked, "What is the path?" or in Chinese, "What is the Tao?" he replied, "Walk on." In other words, "Go." But you can't really go in the first place until you can sit all in one place. And one of the old masters said, "Walk or sit as you will, but whatever you do, don't wobble."

PART TWO

1963–1965

CHAPTER FOUR

MYSTICISM AND MORALITY

WHEN I USE THE WORD *MYSTICISM* I am referring to a kind of experience — a state of consciousness, shall we say — that seems to me to be as prevalent among human beings as measles. It is something that simply happens. And we don't know why it happens. All sorts of techniques claim to promote it and are more or less successful in doing so, but there is a peculiar thing that does happen to people. It is an experience that can actually be described from a number of quite different points of view, but we could add them up to a few dominant characteristics.

One ordinarily feels that one is a separate individual in confrontation with a world that is foreign to one's self, that is "not me." In the mystical kind of experience, though, that separate individual finds itself to be of one and the same nature or identity as the outside world. In other words, the individual suddenly no longer feels like a stranger in the world; rather, the external world feels as if it were his or her own body.

The next aspect of the mystical feeling is even more difficult to assimilate into our ordinary practical intelligence. It is the overwhelming sense that everything that happens — everything that I or anybody else has ever done — is part of a harmonious design and that there is no error at all.

Now, I am not talking about philosophy; I am not talking about a rationalization or some sort of theory that somebody cooked up in order to explain the world and make it seem a tolerable place in which to live. I am talking about a rather whimsical, unpredictable experience that suddenly hits people — an experience that includes this feeling of the total harmoniousness of everything.

I realize that those words — *the total harmoniousness of everything* — can carry with them a sort of sentimental or Pollyanna feeling. There are various religions in our society today that try to inculcate the belief that everything is harmonious unity. They want, in a sense, to propagandize the belief that everything is harmonious.

To my mind, that is a kind of pseudomysticism. It is an attempt to make the tail wag the dog or to make the effect produce the cause — because the authentic sensation of the true harmony of things is never brought about by insisting that everything is harmonious. When you do that — when you say to yourself, "All things are light, all things are God, all things are beautiful" — you are actually implying that they are not, because you wouldn't be saying it if you really knew it to be true.

So the sensation of universal harmony cannot come to us when it is sought or when we look for it as an escape from the way we actually feel or as compensation for the way we actually feel. It comes out of the blue. And when it does, it is overwhelmingly convincing. It is the foundation for most of mankind's profound philosophical, mystical, metaphysical, and religious ideas. Someone who has experienced this sort of thing cannot restrain himself. He has to get up and tell everybody about it. And, alas, he becomes the founder of a religion, because people say, "Look at that man, how happy he is, what conviction he has. He has no doubts. He seems so sure in everything he does."

This is the wonderful thing about a great human being. He is like an animal or a flower. When a flower bud opens, it has no hesitation or doubts. When a young woman appears in society as a debutante, she is not quite sure if she is going to come off. She appears on the stage of society with some doubts in her mind. And therefore all appearances of this kind are rather sickly in nature. But when the bird sings, or the chicken egg breaks or a flower buds, there is no doubt about it at all. It just comes forth.

And so, in the same way, when somebody has an authentic mystical experience, it just comes forth. He just has to tell everybody about it, because he notices everybody around him looking dreadfully serious. Looking as if they had a problem. Looking as if the act of living were extremely difficult. But from the standpoint of the person who has had this experience, they look funny. They don't understand that there isn't any problem at all.

The mystic has seen that the meaning of being alive is just to be alive. That is to say, when I look at the color of your hair and the shape of your eyebrow, I understand that their shape and color are their point. And this is what we are all here for, as well: to be. It is so plain and so obvious and so simple. And yet, everybody rushes around in a great panic as if it were necessary to achieve something beyond themselves. The funny thing is, they are not even quite sure what they need to achieve, but they are devilishly intent on achieving it.

To the person who is in the state of consciousness I call mystical, this frenzy of activity all seems very weird, absurd. It is not to be criticized in an unkindly way, however. It's just a pity that they don't see their own absurdity.

One of the funny things about them is that they don't realize that there is a dimension, a sense in which their pursuit is magnificent. Jesus said, "Father, forgive them, for they know not what they do." I want to turn that into its opposite, in a way. I want to bless them — not forgive them — for not knowing what they're doing. I want to honor them, because the intensely serious preoccupations and anxieties of mankind appear to be not only absurd, but also a kind of marvel. They are a marvel in the same way, perhaps, that the protective coloring of a butterfly, which has somehow contrived to make its wings look like enormous eyes, is a marvel. When a bird that is about to devour it is confronted by these staring eyes, it hesitates a little, as you do when somebody stares at you. The butterfly appears to stare at the bird, and this phenomenon — the marvelous staring wings of the butterfly — seems to be a result of anxiety, the anxiety to survive all the problems and struggles of natural selection. And so, in our intense struggle, we are perhaps all unknowing poets.

One of the greatest ideas that has ever been produced is the Hindu idea that the world is a drama in which the central and supreme self behind all existence has gotten lost and has come to believe that it is not the one supreme self, but all the creatures that there are. It has come to believe in its own artistry. And the more involved, the more anxious, the more finite, the more limited the infinite manages to feel itself to be, the greater that artistry, the greater the depth of the illusion that it has created.

All art, in a way, is illusion. The art of the magician is the art of directing illusion, but all art, be it painting or theater, relies on illusions.

And so, the more anxiety there is, the more uncertainty there is, the more the universe has succeeded with its artistry. Just as when you are watching a play or reading a novel or viewing a movie, the more the author or actor manages to persuade you that the movie or novel is reality, the more he or she has succeeded as an artist. You may retain a faint recognition in the back of your mind that a play, for instance, is only a play. But when you are sitting on the edge of your seat and you are sweating and your hands are clutching the arms of the chair because the scene grips you, that play is magnificent art.

The Hindus feel that the whole arrangement of the cosmos is exactly like that: When in actual life you are wondering whether your doctor is a competent surgeon or charlatan, or whether your investments are good or bad, the Hindus believe that all those feelings of crisis are exactly the same as the feelings you experience when you are sitting in the theater. As the Hindus would say, that thing in you that is real and that connects you under the surface with every other living being — that thing is the player of all the parts. It is the creator of the illusion. It is the source of the game that has got you so involved. And it is living it up in the same way the actors on the stage are living it up — and for the same reason: to convince you that the game is reality.

Everybody loves to play this game — the game of hide-and-seek, the game of scaring oneself with uncertainty. It is human. It is why we go to the theater or movies and why we read novels. And our so-called real life, seen from the position of the mystic, is a version of the same thing. The mystic is the person who has realized that the game is a game. It is hide-and-seek, and everything associated with the "hide" side of it is connected to those places within us where we as individuals feel lonely, impotent, put down, and so on — the negative side of existence.

I have tried at various times to show that there is really one simple principle that underlies everything: All insides have outsides. You don't know that the inside is an inside unless there is an outside. And you don't know that the outside is an outside unless there is an inside.

You — as you ordinarily experience yourself — are an inside. You are the animate, sensitive being inside your skin. But the inside of the skin goes with the outside of the skin. If there weren't an outside of the skin, there wouldn't be an inside. And the outside of the skin is the whole cosmos — galaxy after galaxy and everything else. And it goes with the inside in the same way that front goes with back. If you understand that, then you will truly feel the harmoniousness of everything. And that is the mystic's point of view.

Now, if I may switch subjects a little, what is morality?

Morality refers to a set of rules that are analogous to the rules of language. It is perfectly obvious that we can talk to each other in English, for instance, only if there is mutual agreement among ourselves as to how to use the language — what words refer to what experiences and how words are to be strung together so as to be useful and meaningful. It is interesting that we humans don't have much trouble in coming to this agreement about language. The police don't have to enforce grammar. The schoolteacher — yes — the schoolteacher sometimes has to enforce grammar with students and say in an authoritative way that they must use the correct grammatical forms. But when we grow up, we use these grammatical forms without much difficulty.

Just as we have to agree in order to communicate about language, we also have to agree about the rules of driving on the highway, the rules of doing business, the rules of banking, the rules of family arrangements, and so on. These rules are of the same kind as the rules of grammar. But, alas, this similarity is not often recognized, because the authority, the sanctions, the power behind these rules is different from the authority that underlies grammar. What I mean is this: If you transgress the rules of grammar, people just shrug their shoulders and say, "Well, he isn't making sense." They won't summon the police. But if you transgress the rules of the highway, or of finances, someone is likely to call the cops. One senses the authority of the state behind those rules.

There are other rules that have behind them the authority of, not the state, but the Lord God Almighty. And if you transgress those rules, you are in danger, not simply of going to jail, but, depending on your religious persuasion, of frying forever in hell. At the very least, you have shown yourself, lamentably, to be nothing better than a real person.

Now, wherever the domains of mysticism and morality come into conflict, there is a problem. Throughout the history of religion, mystics have always been suspect. Religions and their priests have been the upholders of moral rules. They have been the guardians of moral authority in the same way as lexicographers or grammarians have been the guardians of the rules of language. But when the mystical experience appears within the domain of religion, the priests always become very disturbed.

For example, recently in California there has been a strange outbreak within the Episcopal Church. Various congregations have experienced a phenomenon called *glossolalia*, which means "speaking in tongues."

If you turn on your radio on a Sunday night to any African-American revival meeting, you will hear glossolalia. The preacher begins by talking sensibly, but then, as the congregation gets more and more enthusiastic, saying, "Amen, Yes, Lord. Teach on that," the preacher works himself up to the point where he isn't talking sense anymore. He's just wailing, shouting, and celebrating the glorious nonsense of the universe.

In other words, all the dry, theological categories become poetry, as well as something beyond poetry: music. The preacher has become at that moment as one with the universe, because he is doing exactly what the stars are doing. The stars above and the galaxies are not making sense. They are just pouring out into the sky in a colossal display of fireworks.

Well, in recent months, various congregations of the Episcopal Church have had outbreaks of glossolalia. The Bishop of California, Bishop Pike, wrote an encyclical letter to his pastors that said, in effect, we must not be too dogmatic. We must recognize always that the spirit of God may work in mysterious ways that cannot be foreseen. We should keep an open mind about all these matters. This message was presented in a very complicated way, requiring several pages. But then, despite those sentiments, when it came to the question of the validity of speaking in tongues, the encyclical said, in no uncertain terms, *this must not happen in the Episcopal Church.* There was an iron hand in Bishop Pike's velvet glove.

This has been the characteristic attitude of priests and guardians of law and order throughout the ages. Everything, as they say in the Episcopal Church, should be done decently and in order.

The guardians of this kind of law and order have always been afraid of the spontaneous manifestations of the spirit. Not simply of things like mysticism, but also of things like falling in love. This leads to an absolutely astounding paradox. We know that human love is genuine only when it is felt in the depth of the heart. And we know that this is true whether it be love for another human or love of God. And, of course, we are always looking to receive genuine love. We don't want others to love us because they are forced to. We want them to love us because they really do love us in their hearts.

When you study the history of the Hebrews, which underlies Christianity, you will discover two traditions constantly compensating for one another and playing off each other: the priestly tradition and the prophetic tradition. The priesthood is concerned with the external observance of laws. The prophetic tradition is concerned with the internal motivations behind actions. Prophets constantly condemn the meaningless adherence to law as hypocritical. In this sense, Jesus is the greatest of the prophets. Even if a man has never committed adultery, the prophet says that if he has looked at a woman with lust, he has already committed adultery in his heart. To really obey the law, in other words, you must obey it with your feelings and not just outwardly. For as Jeremiah says, "The day will come when no man shall any more say to his brother, 'Know God' — that is to say, 'know the law of God' — but they shall all know me, for I will write my law in their inward parts."

The ideal, in other words, is the person who does not simply obey the rules, but whose desires are transformed from the heart. To have the law written on the heart means to change one's desire.

And this peculiarly paradoxical situation exists within the established Church: being required or forced by law to be loving, while at the same time being required to feel that love in one's heart.

This is where the astonishing conflict between the mystic and moralist occurs. For the mystic knows that he has to be more than the legalist. He has to do more than outwardly observe the law. Luther said that the law that requires inward compliance is the most terrible thing. A great deal of his philosophy was an attack on the idea that one's inner feelings could be commanded, because the moment you subscribe to the idea that your inner feelings should be commanded, you open the door to hypocrisy. If you tell others that you love them simply because you know you are supposed to love them, but in your heart, you don't love them at all, then you are a liar and a hypocrite. And the more you insist on that lie — and the more you feel it is your duty to change your feelings and love others — the deeper and deeper you get into trouble. The truth will come out. You will not be able to sustain the pretense. You will not have sufficient energy to go on pretending and making a mockery of the feeling of love. And, if you are honest, you will have to say at last, "I don't love." It doesn't matter whether you have to say this to some other human being or, in a religious situation, if you have to sit back and say to the Lord, "Lord, I don't love you. I think you are a bore. You are demanding. You are authoritarian. You are domineering. I probably ought to love you, but I don't."

Now, we are afraid that an honest expression of our feelings would be disruptive to law and order. But it wouldn't. Not in the least. Actually it would contribute to law and order.

I was once associated in a business way with somebody who was a complicated person. He always pretended that he was a great idealist and that whatever he was doing was for the benefit of mankind, for the furtherance of mutual understanding, and to promote unselfishness and love between human beings. Actually, his dealings were very shady ethically. And I couldn't get along with him, because he wouldn't come clean. If he had said, "Look, I'm in a jam, and in order to get around it, I need you to manipulate things with me thus and so. I know this isn't ethical, but this is what I need you to do." I would have said, "Well, I'm entirely in agreement with you." If he hadn't come on in his usual pious way, which I found sickening and offensive, but had come on in a human way, we would have understood each other.

This example shows that real honesty is a genuine basis for morality. Real honesty means not pretending that your feelings are other than they are. Sometimes we may have to do things that go against our feelings. For example, you may have to help people whom you don't like and you don't want to help. Don't be dishonest. Don't say that your feelings are different from what they are.

Now we can perhaps understand something about the deep relationship between morals and mysticism. If we go back to the mystical experience that I described earlier in terms of the harmoniousness of everything, we can see that such harmony applies to human behavior, too. Its ups and downs are no different in principle from the behavior of the clouds or the wind or dancing flames in a fireplace.

When you watch the pattern of the dancing flames, you see that they never do anything vulgar. Their artistry is always perfect.

Ultimately, it is the same with human beings. We are just as much a part of the natural order as flames in the fire or stars in the sky. But this is only apparent to the person who is honest, in the sense in which I have been using that word. The person who is tied up with trying to pretend that his feelings are other than what they actually are can never see this. He will always be a troublemaker. He is the original hypocrite. The one who is most destructive is the person who pretends to be a model of love and rectitude and justice, when in fact he isn't. And nobody really can be. Altogether superior to the hypocrite is the person I call the loving cynic, who knows of course that everybody has weaknesses, but who isn't contemptuous of anyone for that reason.

A book that illuminates the mind of a loving cynic is *Memories, Dreams, and Reflections* by C. G. Jung. It is the autobiography of a man who was a superb human being, in the particular sense of thoroughly knowing his own limitations and having a sense of humor about it. Jung was a man who understood how to integrate into his being the devilish and compulsive aspects of his nature.

In the metaphysical sphere, the mystic is the one who feels that everything that happens is in some way right, is in some way an integral, harmonious part of the universe. Now, when we transplant or translate that idea into the moral sphere, the sphere of human conduct, the equivalent insight is this: There are no wrong feelings. There may be wrong actions, in the sense of actions contrary to the rules of human behavior. But the way you feel toward other people — loving them, hating them, and so on — is never wrong. And it's absurd and dishonest to try and force your feelings to be other than they are.

The idea that there are no wrong feelings is immensely threatening to people who are afraid to feel. This is one of the peculiar problems of Western culture: We are terrified of our feelings, because they take off on their own. We think that if we give them any scope, if we don't immediately beat them down, they will lead us into all kinds of chaotic and destructive actions.

It is funny that we in our Western culture today believe this — we who do more chaotic and reckless things than any culture has ever done before. If, instead, we would accept our feelings and look upon their comings and goings as something that is as beautiful and as natural and as necessary as changes in the weather or the sequence of night and day or the four seasons, we would be at peace with ourselves. Because what has been problematic for Western man is not so much his struggles with other people and their needs and problems, but rather his struggles with his own feelings — with what he will allow himself to feel and what he won't allow himself to feel. He is ashamed to feel profoundly sad. It is unmanly to cry. He is ashamed to loathe somebody, because he has been told not to hate people. He is ashamed to be overcome with the beauty of something — whether a natural landscape or a member of the opposite sex — because being overcome means not being in control. As a result of this repression, he ends up going out of his mind. We are always out of control when we don't accept our feelings, when we try to pretend that our inner life is different from what it really is.

The most releasing thing that anybody can possibly understand is that our inner feelings are never wrong. They may not be a
correct guide to how we should act, of course. If you feel that you
hate someone intensely, it isn't necessarily right to go up to that
person and cut his throat. But it is right that you should have the
feeling of hate. For you see, when a person comes to himself, he
comes to be one with his own feelings. And that is the only way to
control them.

The sailor always keeps the wind in his sail. Whether he wants
to sail with the wind or against it, he always uses the wind. He
never denies the wind.

In the same way, a person has to keep in contact with his own
feelings. Whether he wants to act as his feelings obviously suggest
or in a different way, he still has to keep his feelings with him,
because they are his own essential self. As soon as he abandons his
feelings, he has lost himself. He becomes an empty mask with no
reality behind it. And all his protestations of love and goodwill will
be hollow.

If a woman has a child conceived by accident, she may think,
"I really didn't want to have this baby, and I don't want the responsibility, but I mustn't think those thoughts. All good mothers love
their babies." And so she says to her child, "I love you." But her
milk is sour, and the baby becomes confused.

It would be much better if the mother said to the baby, "Listen,
you are a pest and a nuisance, and I didn't want you." Then
they would understand each other. Everything would be clear.
There would be no confusions, and no one would feel mixed up.
And because when you feel that somebody is a pest and a nuisance,
and you tell him so, you are apt, after a while, to develop a kind of
humorous feeling about your irritation with him. After a while, you
might even start saying, "You old bastard" with a kind of affection.

The point is that, through their honesty, both the adult and child keep in touch with their true feelings, and instead of denying a difficult situation, they face it, and may in fact grow out of it.

So, what the mystic feels while in the mystical state of mind is the divinity, the glory, of everything that is. And when we apply that mystical insight to the moral sphere, it is one's genuine feelings that are divine and glorious. Therefore, these genuine feelings must always be admitted, must always be allowed. Let me emphasize once more that this doesn't mean that we are therefore always compelled to act upon our feelings — to kill the person we hate, for instance. On the contrary, conscious hatred need not lead to violence at all. In fact, it is most often unconscious hatred that leads to violence. What I am saying is that it is the recognition and acceptance of what one honestly feels that is the moral equivalent of the mystic's vision of the divinity of existence.

CHAPTER FIVE

THE IMAGES OF MAN

I WANT TO START by giving what may be a new definition of myth. Normally *myth* means tale, a fable, a falsehood, or an idea that is out-of-date, something untrue. But another older, stricter use of the word means not something untrue, but rather an image in terms of which people make sense of life and the world. For example, suppose you do not understand the technicalities of electricity, and somebody wanted to explain about the flow of currents. He might compare electricity to water, and because you understand water, you may get some idea about the behavior of electricity. An astronomer explaining what he means by expanding space will use the metaphor of a balloon, a black balloon with white spots on it. The white spots represent the galaxies, and if you blow up the balloon, they all get farther away from each other at the same speed as the balloon blows up. We are not saying that electricity is water, or that the universe is the balloon with white spots on it, but that they are something like that.

In the same way, the human being has always used images to

represent his deepest ideas of the working of the universe, and man's place in it. I am going to discuss certain aspects of two of the greatest myths, in this sense of the word, that have influenced mankind's thinking. First is the myth of the universe as an artifact, something made as a carpenter makes tables, chairs, houses, or as a potter makes pots, or a sculptor makes figurines. The other is the image of the world as a drama, in which all the things in the world are not made but acted, in the same way as a player acts parts. These are the two great images that govern respectively the religions of the West descended from Hebraism — Hebraism itself, Christianity, Islam — and the religions of the East, with their origin in India: Hinduism in particular, and to a lesser extent, Buddhism.

I want to make it perfectly plain, before I go any further, that in talking about these two great religious traditions in terms of images, I am talking about the way they express themselves at a rather popular level. Sophisticated Christians and Hindus think beyond images. For example, a Christian may think of God as the father, but a sophisticated and educated Christian does not imagine that God is a cosmic male parent with a white beard sitting on a golden throne above the stars. Nor does a Hindu imagine literally that God is the super showman, the big actor. These images are what it is like, not what it is, and perhaps when I get through with discussing them we will be able to ask whether any of these images still make sense to us in this twentieth century, when we have a view of the world so powerfully shaped by Western science.

I begin with a few aspects of the image of the world, and thus the image of man, as it comes to us from the Hebrew Bible. It says in the Book of Genesis that the Lord God created man out of the dust of the earth, as if He had made a clay figure of Adam. He blew the breath of life into its nostrils and the figurine became alive. It says that the figurine was made in the image of God. God, who is conceived in this particular image as a personal, living, intelligent spirit, creates in man something similar. This is very definitely a creation, as the potter makes a pot out of clay. For the creature that the Lord God has made is not God. The creature is something less than God, something like God but not God.

Some very interesting consequences follow from this idea of the world as an artifact. What follows is that the whole universe is seen as a marvelous technological accomplishment. If it was created, there must be an explanation of how it was made, and the whole history of Western thought has in many ways been an attempt to discover how the creator did it. What were the principles? What laws were laid down? What is the blueprint that underlies this creation? This image has persisted throughout Western history, and continues on into a time when very many people do not believe in Christianity, or Judaism, or Islam. They are agnostics or atheists, but they still carry with them something of this idea of the world as an artifact. If you are a Christian or a Jew, you believe that the world is an artifact of creation of the intelligent spirit called God. But if you are an atheist or an agnostic in this culture, you believe that the world is an automatic machine without a creator, something that made itself.

We might say that our original model of the universe was the ceramic model. The Bible is full of references to God as the potter who makes the world out of obedient clay. And even when Western thinkers in the eighteenth century began to drop the idea of a personal God, they still kept the idea of the artifact. So we could say that after the ceramic model of the universe, we got the fully automatic model.

Underlying our way of thinking about things is the question, How are they put together? And if you want to find out, one of the obvious ways to proceed is to take them to pieces. Everybody knows that if you want to find out how something is made, you unscrew the parts and see what the secret is inside the box. So Western science in its beginnings took everything apart. It took animals apart; it took flowers apart; it took rocks apart.

When they got everything reduced to its tiniest pieces, they tried to find methods for taking those apart, too, so that we could eventually discover what the very smallest things were, and learn what method the creator, or the fully automatic universe, used in putting everything together. It was hoped that this would lead us to an understanding of how life works. Man himself was also looked on as a creation, as something that had been made. But there were some difficulties with this idea, because if you believe in the world in accordance with the fully automatic model, you really have got to admit that man, too, must be fully automatic, a machine rather than a person. Man, then, doffs his hat and says, "How do you do? I am a person. I am alive. I am sensible. I talk, I have feelings." But you wonder, "Does he really, or is he just an automaton?"

Under the dispensation of the fully automatic model, the Western image of man is that we are very sensitive, living beings, and that inside the human skin, by an extraordinary fluke of nature, there has arisen something called reason. There have also arisen "values," such as love. But these were flukes because they happened inside a fully automatic universe that, because it is merely automatic, must be stupid. In other words, you won't find anything really intelligent outside human skins. Therefore, the only thing that people can do if they want to maintain reason and love in this universe is to fight nature, and beat the stupid, external world into submission to the human will. So the war against nature is the great project of Western technology thus far, because each one of us has inherited from thousands of years of history a view of man as something made of breath breathed into a pot of clay. Each one feels himself to be a globule of consciousness or mind living inside a vehicle called "my body." Since the world outside that body is stupid, we feel estranged from the world.

When we find out how enormous the universe is, that makes us feel extremely unimportant and rather lonely, because our basic image of ourselves is of a soul, an ego, a mind by itself in its little house, looking out at a world that is strange, and saying, "That is not me." I am therefore a brief interval of consciousness between the darkness and the darkness. That is not too happy a thought. I would like to be able to believe that there is more to life than that. Many of us say, "If only I could believe that there is an intelligent and eternal God in whose eyes I am important, and who has the power to enable me to live forever, that would be very nice." But for many people that is an extraordinarily difficult thing to believe.

I want to contrast this ceramic image of the world with the distinctly different dramatic image that is the presiding image of the Hindus. Their idea is that God did not make the world, but acted it. That is to say, every person and every thing is a role or part that the Godhead is playing. Of course, the Hindu image of God is a little bit different from the Jewish, the Christian, and the Islamic image. When I was a little boy, I used to ask my mother interminable questions. When she got sick of it, she said, "My dear, there are some things in life that we are just not meant to know." And I said, "Will we ever know?" And she said, "Yes, if you die and then go to heaven, God will explain it all."

I used to hope that on rainy afternoons in heaven we would all sit around the throne of grace and ask the Lord, "Why did you do this?" and "Why did you do that?" And He would explain.

Every child in the West asks his mother, "How was I made?" No person knows, but we think that perhaps God knows, and He will be able to explain. Likewise, if anybody becomes mentally deranged and claims to be God, we always humor such people by asking them technical questions, "How did you make the world in six days?" or, "If you are God, why couldn't you change this plate into a rabbit?" We do this because, in our popular image of God, God is the supreme technocrat. He knows all the answers. He understands everything in detail and can tell you all about it.

The Hindus don't think of God that way. If you ask the Hindu God, "How did you create the human body?" He would say, "I know how I did it, but it can't be explained in words because words are too clumsy. In words I have to talk about things slowly. I have to string them out, because words run in a line, and lines add up to books, and books add up to libraries. If I explain to you how I made the human organism, it will take all eternity. I don't have to understand things in words in order to make them happen. Nor do you." You don't have to understand in words how to breathe. You just breathe. You don't have to understand in words how to grow your hair, how to shape your bones, how to make your eyes blue or brown, you just do it. And somebody who does understand to some extent — a physiologist, perhaps — can't do it any better than you.

That is the Hindu idea of divine omnipotence, and that is why their images of the gods very often have many arms. You will often see the god Shiva with ten arms, or the Buddhist Avalokiteshvara with one thousand arms. Their image of the divine is of a sort of centipede. A centipede can move a hundred legs without having to think about it, and Shiva can move ten arms very dexterously without having to think about them. You know what happened to the centipede when it stopped to think how to move a hundred legs; it got all balled up. So the Hindus do not think of God as being a technician in the sense of having a verbal or mathematical understanding of how the world is created. It is just done simply, like that. If we had to describe this simple way in words it would be very complicated, but God, in the Hindus' idea, does not need to do so.

The Hindu does not see any fundamental division between God and the world. The world is God at play; the world is God acting. How did they arrive at such an idea? Very simply. When you try to think about why there is a world at all, you realize it is extraordinarily odd that there should be anything. It would have been much simpler and would have required a great deal less energy for there to have been nothing. But here everything is. Why? Well, what would you do if you were God? Suppose that every night you could dream any dream you wanted. What would you dream? I am quite sure that most of us would dream of all the marvelous things we wanted to have happen to us. We would fulfill all our wishes. We might go on that way for months, and we could make it extraordinarily rich by dreaming seventy-five years full of glorious happenings in one night.

After you had done that for a few months, though, you might begin to get a little tired of it and say, "What about an adventure tonight, in which something terribly exciting and rather dangerous is going to happen? But I will know I am dreaming so it won't be too bad, and I'll wake up if it gets too serious." So you do that for a while; you rescue princesses from dragons, and all sorts of things. Then after doing that for some time, you might say, "Let's go a bit further. Let's forget it's a dream, and have a real thrill." Ooh! But you know you will wake up. Then, after you have done that for a while, you will dare yourself to get out as far as you can, and you will end up dreaming the life you are living right now.

The reason for this, the Hindu would say, is that the basic pulse of life, the basic motivation of existence, is like the game of hide-and-seek. Now you see it, now you don't. Everything is based on that; all life is vibration, pulsation. Light is a pulsation of light and dark. Sound is a pulsation of sound and silence. Everything is going back and forth at various speeds. The motion of a wave consists of two pulses, the crest and the trough. You can't have crests without troughs; you can't have troughs without crests. They always go together. You can't have hide without seek; you can't have seek without hide. You can't have here without there; if you didn't know where there was, you wouldn't know where here was. You can't have is without isn't, because you don't know what you mean by is unless you also know what you mean by isn't, and vice versa.

Hide-and-seek is the fundamental game of the universe, in the Hindu view. It is as if the Lord God, or Brahman, had said in the beginning, "Get lost, man. Disappear. I'll find you again later." When the disappearance gets very far out, the contrary rhythm begins, the dreamer wakes up and says, "Whoo, that's a relief." Then after a period of rest, in which everything is at peace, it starts all over again. The spirit of adventure springs eternal.

The Hindus, for their period in history, had extremely vast ideas of space and time. They had the theory that the hiding part of the universal game goes on for 4,320,000 years, a period called a *kalpa* in Sanskrit. The "dreaming" part is followed by the "waking" part. The dreaming is the hiding where the Godhead imagines that it is all of us. Then for another 4,320,000 years there is a period of awakening, and at the end of that begins the dream again. The dreaming period is further subdivided into four stages. The first stage is the longest, and it is the best. During that stage, the dream is beautiful. The second stage is not quite so long, and is a little unsettling. There is an element of instability in it, a certain touch of insecurity. In the third stage, which is shorter still, the forces of light and the forces of darkness — or good and evil — are equally balanced, and things are beginning to look rather dangerous. In the fourth stage, the shortest of them all, the negative, dark, or evil side triumphs, and the whole thing blows up in the end. But that is like the bang in a dream when you get shot, and you wake up, and see it was just a dream after all. There is a waking period, and then the whole thing starts again.

You will notice, if you make the computation, that in this drama the forces of the dark side are operative for one-third of the time; the forces of the light side for two-thirds of the time. This is a very ingenious arrangement; we see in it the fundamental principles of drama. Suppose this is not a lecture tonight but a show. There are actors coming on the stage, but they are real people like you. In order for you not to see them in that way, they are going to put on their costumes and makeup, and then they are going to come out in front here and pretend to various roles. And you know you want to be half-convinced that what they are doing on the stage is real. The work of a great actor is to get you sitting on the edge of your chair, anxious, or weeping, or roaring with laughter, because he had almost persuaded you that what is on the stage is really happening. That is the greatness of his art, to take the audience in.

In the same way, the Hindu feels that the Godhead acts his part so well that he takes himself in completely. And each one of you is the godhead, wonderfully fooled by your own act. And although you won't admit it to yourself, you are enjoying it like anything.

When you say, "I am a person," the word *person* is from the drama. When you open a play script and see the list of the actors, this is the dramatis personae, the persons of the drama. The word *person* in Latin is *persona*, meaning "through sound," or something through which sound comes; the persona in Greek or Roman drama was the mask worn by the actors. And because they acted on an open-air stage, the mask's mouth was shaped like a small megaphone that would project the sound. So the person is the mask. Isn't it funny how we have forgotten that? Harry Emerson Fosdick could write a book called *On Being a Real Person*, which translated literally is, "How to be a genuine fake," because in the old sense, the person is the role, the part played by the actor. But if you forget that you are the actor, and think you are the person, you have been taken in by your own role. You are "en-rolled," or bewitched, spellbound, enchanted.

Something else about the nature of drama is that there must be a villain, unless of course you are acting some kind of a nonplay that does not have any story. Fundamentally, all stories start out with the status quo. Everybody is just sort of going along, and then some problem comes in to upset everything. The interest of the play lies in the question, How are we going to solve that problem? It is the same when you play cards. If you are playing solitaire, you start by shuffling the deck, introducing chaos. The game is to play order against chaos. In the drama there must be a villain, a dark side, so that the hero can play against him, and it. If you go the theater for a good cry, then you let the villain win and you call it a tragedy. If you go for a thrill, you let the hero win. If you go for laughs, you call it a comedy. There can be various arrangements between the hero and the villain, but when the curtain goes down at the end of the drama, the hero and the villain always step out hand in hand and the audience applauds both. They do not boo the villain at the end of the play. They applaud him for acting the part of the villain so well, and they applaud the hero for acting the part of the hero so well, because they know that the hero and the villain are only roles, masks.

Behind the stage is the green room. After the play is over, and before it begins, the masks are there. The Hindus feel that behind the scene, under the surface of reality, you are all actors, marvelously skilled at playing parts and in getting lost in the mazes of your own minds and the entanglements of your own affairs, as if this were the most urgent thing going on. But behind the scenes, in the green room — in the very back of your mind and the very depth of your soul — you always have a sneaking suspicion that you might not be the you that you think you are. The Germans call this a *hintergedanke*, a thought way back in your head that you will hardly admit to yourself, because if you were brought up in the Hebrew-Christian tradition, it would be very wicked indeed to think that you were God. That would be blasphemy; and don't you ever dare think such an idea! Of course this is all as it should be, because the show must go on until the time does come to stop.

Now you will see that these different images of the universe involved two quite different ways of dealing with two fundamental questions. The first question is, What is man? That is, Who are you? In the Hebrew-Christian answer, we more or less say, "I'm me. I am Alan Watts, John Doe, or Mary Smith, and I firmly believe that's who I am, because I really oughtn't think anything else, ought I?" And this "me" is a finite ego, or a finite mind, whatever that is. On the other hand, the Hindu will say that atman is what we really are. We're the works, the which for which there is no whicher, the root and ground of the universe and of reality.

The next question answered differently by the two traditions is, Why have things gone wrong? Why is there evil; why is there pain; why is there tragedy? In the Christian tradition you must attribute evil to something besides God. God is defined as good, and He originally created the scheme of things without any evil in it. However, in a mysterious accident, one of the angels, called Lucifer, did not do what he was told. And there was the Fall of Man. Man disobeyed, and went against the law of God, and from that point on evil was introduced into the scheme of things and things began to go wrong, in defiance of the will of the perfectly good creator.

The Hindu thinks in a different way. He feels that the creator or the actor is the author of both good and evil because, as I explained, you have to have the evil for there to be a story. In any case, it is not as if the creator had made evil and made someone else its victim. This is not saying, "God creates the evil as well as the good, and he inflicts evil upon us poor little puppets." The Hindu says, "Nobody experiences pain except the Godhead." You are not some separate little puppet who is being kicked around by omnipotence. You are omnipotence in disguise. So there is no victim of this, no helpless, defenseless, poor little thing. Even a baby with an incurable disease is the dreaming Godhead.

This viewpoint makes people brought up in the West extremely uneasy, because it seems to undercut the foundations of moral behavior. They say, "If good and evil are created by God, isn't this a universe in which anything goes? If I realize that I am God in disguise, I can get away with murder." But think it through. Didn't I point out that in the game as the Hindus analyze it, the evil part has one-third of the time and the good part has two-thirds? You will find out that all good games, games worth playing, that arouse our interest, are constructed like this. If you have the good and the evil equally balanced, the game is boring; nothing happens, it is a stalemate. The irresistible force meets the immovable object. On the other hand, if it is mostly good and there is hardly any evil, maybe just a teenie little fly in the ointment, it also gets boring. For example, suppose you knew the future, and could control it perfectly. What would you do? You would say, "Let's shuffle the deck and have another deal." When great chess players sit down to a match and it suddenly becomes apparent to both of them that white is going to mate in sixteen moves and nothing can be done about it, they abandon the game and begin another. They do not want to continue if they already know the outcome. There would not be any "hide," any element of surprise, if they knew. Again, good and evil equally balanced is not a good game, and a game with positive or good forces clearly triumphant is not an interesting game. What we want is a game where it always seems that the good side is about to lose, is in really serious danger of losing, but then always manages to sneak out a victory. In serial stories, at the end of every installment the hero is always in some absolutely impossible position — he's going to be run over by a train, and he's tied with his girlfriend to the rails. You know the author is going to get him out of his difficulty, but he mustn't do it too obviously, because that would be boring, and you wouldn't keep reading the installments. So what is necessary is a system in which the good side is always winning but is never the winner, where the evil side is always losing but is never the loser. That is a very practical arrangement for a game that will keep everybody interested.

Watch this principle at work in practical politics. Every in-group of nice people finds that it needs an out-group of nasty people so that its members will know who they are. If you are part of the in-group, you must recognize that the out-group is your necessary enemy, whom you need. Therefore you mustn't obliterate it, because if you do you are in a very dangerous state of affairs. So you have to love your enemies, and regard them as highly necessary adversaries to be respected. We need our enemies and they need us. The thing is to cool it and maintain what I call a contained conflict. When conflicts get out of hand, all sides blow up. Of course I suppose even then there will be another game, in maybe a million years.

Now, let me put these visions of the world together. If you believe the Christian, Hebrew, and Islamic view, you can't admit the Hindu view, because if you are an orthodox Christian, and orthodox Protestant Bible type, or a Roman Catholic, the one thing you cannot believe is that you are God. But let us go back to Judaism for a minute and ask the question, "If Judaism is the true religion, can Christianity also be true?" No, because the one thing in Christianity the Jew cannot admit is that Jesus Christ was God. It is unthinkable for a Jew that any man was indeed God in the flesh.

The next question, then, is, If Christianity is the true religion, can Judaism also be true? The answer is yes, because all Christians are Jews. They have accepted the Jewish religion — in the form of the Old Testament — into their own religion. Every Christian is a Jew with a particular attitude toward Jesus of Nazareth.

Let's play this game once again and ask, "If Christianity is true, can Hinduism also be true?" The answer is no, because the Christians will say, "Jesus of Nazareth was God, but you are not."

The final question is, If Hinduism is true, can Christianity be true as well? The answer is yes, because it can include Christianity. But how? What attitude would a Hindu have toward a very sincere and convinced Christian? He would say, "Bravo, absolutely marvelous; what an actor! Here in this Christian soul God is playing His most extraordinary game. He is believing and feeling that He is not Himself, and not only that, but He is living only one life, and in that life He has got to make the most momentous decision imaginable." In the course of the Christian's four score years and ten, he must choose between everlasting beatitude and everlasting horror. And he is not quite sure how to do it, because in Christianity there are two sins, among others, to be avoided. One is called presumption: knowing surely that you are saved. The other is despair: knowing surely that you are damned. There is always a margin of doubt about being damned or saved, so you work out your salvation in fear and trembling.

Thus Christianity is preeminently the gambler's religion. Imagine you know at some great casino, late at night, that there is some marvelous master gambler who has been winning, winning, winning all night. Then suddenly he decides to stake his whole winnings on whether the ball lands on red or black. Everybody gathers from all over the casino to watch this terrific gamble. In the same way, the predicament in which the Christian soul finds itself is this colossal gamble, in a universe that might possibly contain within it ultimate tragedy, an absolute, final, irremediable mistake. What a horror that thought is! So the Hindu is sitting in the audience fascinated by this Christian's extraordinary gamble. He says, "That's a beautiful game." The Christian does not know it is a game, but the Hindu suspects it is. And he is a little bit admiring of it, but not quite involved.

Perhaps you would say, "Once to every man and nation comes the moment to decide, in the strife twixt truth and falsehood, for the good or evil side. Then it is the brave man chooses while the coward stands aside." That old song sounds great, doesn't it? Commitment; stand up and be counted. This is a virtue, but on the other hand, there is another virtue, which is called being a good sport. If your enemy in the battle of life is to be regarded as an absolute enemy, pure evil as black as black can be, you cannot be a good sport and you can accord him no chivalry, no honors of battle. You have to annihilate him by any means possible, fair or foul. And that leads to some pretty sticky situations, especially when he has the means of annihilating you in just the same way.

If, on the other hand, in all contests you know that while you are going to take it seriously and regard it as very important, in the back of your mind you know it is not ultimately important. Although it is very important, you are saved, and this enables you to be a good player. You may worry about the word *play* because we often use that word in a trivial sense: "You're just playing. You mean life is nothing but a game." The Hindus indeed call the creation of the universe the *lila*, or the game, or the play of the divine. But we, too, use *play* in more profound senses. When you see *Hamlet*, which is by no means trivial, you are still seeing a play. In church the organist plays the organ. And in the Book of Proverbs, it is written that the divine wisdom created the world by playing before the throne of God. When we play music — even the music of Bach, to name a great master of what we call serious music — we are still playing.

The Hindus see this world as "play," in the deeper sense of the word, and therefore they see the intense situations, personally, socially, and so on, in which we are all involved, not as bad illusions but as magnificent illusions, so well acted that they have got most of the actors fooled into forgetting who they are. When he has become fooled, man thinks of himself as a little creature that has come into this strange and foreign world, and is just a little puppet of fate. He has forgotten that the whole thing has, at its root, a playful self that is also your own self.

CHAPTER SIX

THE RELEVANCE
OF ORIENTAL PHILOSOPHY

WESTERN THEOLOGY has not had a very distinguished record in promoting the study of other than the Christian religion, and most study of comparative religion that has gone on in theological schools historically has been missionary oriented, although this is rather puzzling. The student of theology has always been encouraged to investigate the weird ideas of the opposing prospects so as to be able to undermine them. But if you believe in the first place that yours is the only true religion, is there really any point in studying any other one? You could very quickly find reasons for showing the others to be inferior because that was a foregone conclusion — they had to be — because in all the arguments about the respective merits of various religions, the judge and the advocate are the same. If, for example, Christians get into discussions as to whether Jesus Christ was a more profound and spiritual character than the Buddha, they arrive at their decision on the basis of a scale of values that are, of course, Christian. And I really do marvel at this Christian imperialism because it prevails even among theological liberals, and in practice it reaches its final absurdity in religionless religion — the doctrine that there is no God and Jesus Christ is his only son. It is at this point that we begin to see the anxiety that, even though we do not generally believe in God anymore, somehow we have still got to be Christians.

Obviously the Church is a very curious organization that must be understood. The inner meaning of the Church, as it works in fact, is a society of the saved, and a society of the saved necessarily requires a society of the not saved. All social groups with claims to some kind of special status must necessarily create aliens and foreigners. St. Thomas Aquinas let the cat out of the bag one day when he said that the saints in heaven would occasionally peer over the battlements into hell and praise God for the just punishment visited upon evildoers. Now, I realize I am not being very fair or very kind to modern theology, but there remains this strange persistence of insisting that our group is the best group, and I feel that there is in this something peculiarly irreligious, and that furthermore it exhibits a very strange lack of faith. One can draw a strong distinction between faith on the one hand, and belief on the other. As a matter of fact, belief is quite contrary to faith. Belief is really wishing, and it comes from the Anglo-Saxon root *lief*, "to wish." As expressed in the Apostles' Creed, belief is a fervent hope, a hope that the universe will turn out to be thus and so. In this sense therefore, belief precludes the possibility of faith. Faith is openness to truth, to reality, whatever it may turn out to be. "I want to know the truth" — that is the attitude of faith. Most Christians use ideas about the universe and about God as something to hang onto in the spirit of "Rock of Ages cleft for me." Hymnal imagery is full of such rocks: "A mighty fortress is our God," "Unharmed upon the eternal rock, the eternal city stands." There is something very rigid about a rock, but we are finding our rock getting rather worn out in an age where it is becoming more and more obvious that our world is a floating world. Ours is a world floating in space where all positions are relative, and any point may be regarded as the center. Our world does not float on anything, and therefore, the religious attitude appropriate to our time is not one of clinging to rocks but of learning how to swim. You know that if you get in the water and have nothing to hold onto, but try to behave as you would on dry land, you will drown. But if, on the other hand, you trust yourself to the water and let go, you will float. And this is exactly the situation of faith.

In the New Testament, when Jesus began to foretell his own death, his disciples became greatly disturbed because it was written in the Law that the Messiah would not die. To this Jesus replied: "Unless a grain of wheat falls into the earth and dies, it remains alone; but if it dies, it brings forth much fruit." There is also the curious incident after the Resurrection when Mary Magdalene, being so delighted to see the Master again, reached out to grab hold of him, and Jesus said, "Do not cling to me!" On another occasion he said to the disciples: "It is expedient for you that I go away, for if I go not away, the Holy Spirit cannot come to you." But somehow we have reversed all this. Jesus, it seems to me, was one of those rare and remarkable individuals who had a particular kind of spiritual experience that, in terms of Hebrew theology, he found most difficult to express without blasphemy. He said, "I and the Father are One"; in other words, "I am God." Now, if you are a Hindu, that is a rather natural statement to make; but in our culture, which has Hebrew theology in its background, anyone who says, "I am God" is either blasphemous or insane. It is our image of God as "Our Father" that really influences our conception of God, and the image has far more emotional power than any amount of theology or abstraction. It is not like Tillich's decontaminated name for God,

"The Ground of Being," nor like Professor Northrop's "Undifferentiated Aesthetic Continuum." These expressions are not very moving, even though subtle theologians prefer such descriptions. They tell us that when we call God "The Father" we do not have to believe literally that he is a cosmic male parent, and still less that he has a white beard and sits on a golden throne above the stars. No serious modern theologian ever believed in such a God. But nevertheless, the image of the monotheistic God of the West affects us because it is political. The title "King of Kings and Lord of Lords" is the title of the emperors of ancient Persia. Our image of God is based on the Pharaohs, on the great rulers of the Chaldeans, and on the kings of Persia; it is the image of the political governor and Lord of the Universe who keeps order and who rules it from, metaphorically speaking, above.

Our image of the world in the West is that the world is a construct, and it is very natural for a child to say to his mother, "How was I made?" as if we were somehow put together. This imagery goes back to Genesis, where the story is told of how God created Adam out of a clay figurine by breathing the breath of life into the nostrils of this figurine, and bringing it to life. This reflects the fundamental supposition that even underlies the development of Western science, which is that everything has been made, that someone knows how it was made, and that you can find out because behind the universe there is an architect. This could be called "the ceramic model of the universe" because it upholds the basic feeling that there are two things in existence: one is "stuff" or material, and the other is form. In our way of thinking material such as clay, by itself, is rather stupid; it has no life in it. So, for matter to assume orderly forms it requires that an external intelligence be introduced to shape it. Now, with that idea deeply embedded in our common sense, it is very difficult for people to realize that this image is not necessarily appropriate for a description of the world. Indeed, the entire concept of "stuff" is strangely absent from modern physics, which looks at the physical universe purely in terms of pattern and structure.

On the other hand, the Hindu model of the universe is a drama. Here the world is not made, it is acted. And behind every face — human, animal, plant, or mineral — there is the face, or non-face, of the central self, the *Atman*, which is Brahman, the final reality that cannot be defined. Obviously, that which is the center cannot be made an object of knowledge any more than you can bite your own teeth, or lift yourself up by your own bootstraps; it is the basis of what there is, and you are it. The idea behind this is that the nature of reality is a game of hide-and-seek, which is really the only game there is — now you see it, now you don't. And this Hindu image is one that is particularly disturbing to Christians because in it is the element of a very special theological profanity called "pantheism." Pantheism is the feeling that every part in the drama of life is being played by the Supreme Lord, and this makes Christians think that all the real distinctions between good and evil are obliterated. But practically speaking, that is the biggest bit of nonsense ever uttered. Distinctions between good and evil do not have to be eternal distinctions to be real distinctions, and to say that a distinction that is not eternal is not real is a highly un-Christian thing to say, and certainly a very un-Jewish thing to say. One of the fundamental principles of the Judeo-Christian attitude is that all finite things that have been created by God are good, and therefore a thing does not have to be infinite to be good. Furthermore, to invoke the authority of heaven in matters of moral regulation is like putting a two-million-volt current through your electric shaver. As the Chinese say, "Do not swat a fly on a friend's head with a hatchet." Like all kinds of judicial torture and harsh justice, such ideas bring law into disrespect. Such a fierce God, and such an unbending attitude, results in people disbelieving in God altogether, and as they say, "throwing out the baby with the bath water." This is one among many reasons why the "God Is Dead" theology arose. It was very inconvenient to have the kind of God who is an authoritarian boss over the world, peering down over your shoulders all the time, knowing your innermost thoughts and judging you. In the so-called "Ages of Faith" people were just as immoral as they are today, so it has never significantly improved anyone's behavior; it is a very uncomfortable feeling, and everyone is happy to be rid of it.

Furthermore, if thou shalt not make any graven image of anything that is in the heavens above, then all these fixed notions of God are idolatrous. The most dangerous and pernicious images are not those made of wood or stone — nobody takes those seriously — they are the images made of imagination, conception, and thought. This is why, in the fundamental approach to the Godhead, both the Hindu and the Buddhist, and for that matter the Taoist, take what is called the negative approach. St. Thomas Aquinas said that to proceed to the knowledge of God, it is necessary to go by the way of remotion — of saying what God is not — since God by his immensity exceeds every conception to which our intellect can attain. When of the Godhead the Hindu says, "All that can truly be said is 'neti, neti,'" or "not this, not this," and when the Buddhist uses such a term for the final reality as shunyata, which means void or emptiness, textbook after textbook on comparative religion by various theologians complain that this is terrible negativism, or nihilism. But it is nothing of the kind. If, for example, you have a window on which there is a fine painting of the sun, your act of faith in the real sun will be to scrape the painting off to let the sun shine in. So, in the same way, pictures of God on the windows of the mind need scraping off, otherwise they become idolatrous substitutes for the reality.

Now, I am hoping that this sort of understanding will issue from the "God Is Dead" theology, but I am not quite sure whether it is going to. As a matter of fact, there are precedents within the Christian tradition for an intelligent theology such as this, for what I would call "atheism in the name of God." In other words, one completely lets go of clinging to images of God because all such images only get in the way of reality. The highest form of prayer is that in which all concepts of God have been left behind — this is the supreme act of faith. But the moment you insist on the Christian image, you support the Church as a huge, imperialistic, vested-interest organization. After all, if the Church is the Body of Christ, is it not through the breaking of the Body of Christ that life is given to the world? But the Church does not want to be broken up, by Jove, no! It goes around canvassing for new members. Consider the difference between a physician and a clergyman. The physician wants to get rid of his patients, so he gives them medicine and hopes they will not get hooked on it; the clergyman, on the other hand, is usually forced to make his patients become addicts so that they will continue to pay their dues. The doctor has faith in turnover; he knows that there will always be sick people. The clergy should also have faith in turnover. Clergymen, get rid of your congregations! Say to your people, "You've heard all I have to tell you. Go away. If you want to get together for making celestial whoopee, which is worship, then all right; but if you come to church out of a sense of duty, you are not wanted." When I was a chaplain at Northwestern University, I used to tell the students that if they did not want to be at Mass they would be only skeletons at the feast, and it would be much better if they stayed in bed or they went swimming, because we were going to celebrate the Holy Communion, and I meant celebrate!

So I think it is a shame that we take religion in such dead earnest. I remember when I was a boy, how wicked I thought it was to laugh in church. We do not realize that, as G. K. Chesterton once said, the angels fly because they take themselves so lightly. So too, in the *Paradiso*, when Dante heard the song of the angels he said it sounded like the laughter of the universe. They were singing, "Alleluia, Alleluia, Alleluia," which does not mean anything; it is sublime nonsense. So in the same way, there are Hindu and Buddhist texts that are the chants of the buddhas, or the divine beings, and that do not mean anything at all and never did. The point that I wish to make most strongly is that behind a vital religious life for the West there has to be a faith that is not expressed as ideas and opinions to which you cling in a kind of desperation. Faith is the act of letting go, and that must begin with letting go of God. This is not atheism in the ordinary sense, because atheism in the ordinary sense is fervently *hoping* that there is no God. But faith is letting God go.

Someone once described "Christian Secularism" as the assumption that there is nothing at all to life except a pilgrimage between the maternity ward and the crematorium, and that it is within that span that Christian concern must be exercised because that is all there is. So I am afraid that this is what the "God Is Dead" movement might evolve into. It is true that this is pretty much common sense these days. I very much doubt whether most religious people really believe in their religion; it has become implausible. Even Jehovah's Witnesses are pretty polite when they come around to the door, but if they really believed what they were talking about they would be screaming in the streets. If Catholics believed what they were talking about they would be making an awful fuss — they would be sponsoring horrendous television programs that would put pro football to shame, and they would have full-page ads in the papers about the terrible things that would happen if "you didn't," and more so if "you did." They would also be very serious about it, but nobody is. And so, it has become extremely plausible that this trip between the maternity ward and the crematorium is what there is to life. We still have going into our common sense the nineteenth-century myth of the universe, which succeeded "the ceramic myth" in Western history. I call it "the myth of the fully automatic model," namely, that it is stupid, blind force. Hegel's phrase "the fortuitous congress of atoms," which is of the same vintage as Freud's libido, is the blind surge of lust at the basis of human psychology. These men of the nineteenth century were indulging in a put-down attitude of the world, and by making it seem as banal as it possibly could be they were advertising their own hardheadedness. This was a kind of role-playing. On the other hand, if we think about the existence of things and our place in the universe, we might be absolutely amazed to discover ourselves on this "ball of rock" rotating around a spherical fire; it is a very odd situation.

The more I look at things, I cannot get rid of the feeling that existence is really quite weird. You see, a philosopher is a sort of intellectual yokel who gawks at things that sensible people take for granted. Sensible people say, "Existence is nothing at all, just go on and do something." So, too, the current movement in philosophy, logical analysis, says you must not even think about existence, it is a meaningless concept. Therefore, philosophy has become the discussion of trivia, and philosophical journals are as satisfactorily dull as any other kind of purely technical inquiry. No good philosopher lies awake at night worrying about the destiny of man and the nature of God because a philosopher today is a practical fellow who goes to the university with his briefcase at nine and leaves at five. He "does" philosophy during the day by discussing whether certain sentences have meaning and, if so, what. However, as William Earle said in a very funny essay, "he would come to work in a white coat if he thought he could get away with it." The problem is that the philosopher of today has lost his wonder, because wonder, in modern philosophy, is something you must not have; it is like enthusiasm in eighteenth-century England — it is very bad form. I wonder about the universe, but it is not a question that I wonder about, it is a feeling that I have. But when I think about it I do not even know what question to ask! What would you ask? Imagine if you had an interview with God and were allowed to ask one question. What would it be? If you do not rush to answer, you will soon find that you have no idea what to ask. I simply cannot formulate the question that contains my wonder. The moment my mouth opens to utter it, I suddenly find I am talking nonsense. Yet this should not prevent wonder from being the foundation of philosophy. As Aristotle said, "Wonder is the beginning of philosophy."

To the philosopher, existence seems very strange, and even more so when he realizes that we are all embraced within a neurological contraption that is able to center itself in the midst of an incredible expanse of galaxies and then start measuring the whole thing. Existence is relationship, and we are smack in the middle of it. Obviously, there is a place in life for a religious attitude in the sense of awe, of astonishment at existence. And this is also a basis of respect for existence — which is something we do not have very much of in this culture, even though we call it materialistic. A materialist is a person who loves material, but in our culture today we are bent on the total destruction of material and its conversion into junk and poisonous gas as quickly as possible. Ours is not a materialistic culture because it has no respect for material. And respect is, in turn, based on wonder — on feeling the marvel of just an ordinary pebble in your fingers.

So I am afraid that the "God Is Dead" theology will sort of drift off into secular do-goodery in the name of Jesus. And this, I think, is where we can be strongly revivified and stimulated by the introduction into our spiritual life of certain things that are Oriental. Now, it must be understood that the crux of the Hindu and Buddhist disciplines is an experience; it is not a theory, nor is it a belief. If we say that a religion is a combination of creed, code, and cult as is true of Judaism, Islam, and Christianity, then Buddhism is not a religion. A creed is a revelation, a revealed symbolism of what the universe is about — and you are commanded to believe in it on divine authority; a code is the revealed will of God for man, which you are commanded to obey. A cult is the divinely revealed form of worship that you must practice. The Ten Commandments must be obeyed because God is boss. He is the ruler, King of Kings and Lord of Lords. But the discipline of yoga in Hinduism, or in the various forms of Buddhist meditation, does not require you to believe anything; they contain no commandments. They do indeed have precepts, but they are really vows that you undertake on your own responsibility, not as an obedience to someone else. They are experimental techniques for changing consciousness, and the thing that they are mainly concerned with is helping human beings to get rid of the hallucination that each one of us is a skin-encapsulated ego — that little man inside our head located between the ears and behind the eyes who is the source of conscious attention and voluntary behavior. Most people do not really think that they are anything but that, and that the body is a thing that you have. "Mommy, who would I have been if my father had been someone else?" as though your parents give you the body and you pop the soul into it at some point — conception or parturition, nobody could ever decide.

This attitude, that we are something in a body, is one that lingers with us. We are taught to experience the beating of the heart as something that happens to us, whereas talking or walking is something that we do. But, do you not beat your heart? Language will not allow you to think that; it is not customary. How do you think? How do you manage to be conscious? Do you know? How do you open and close your hand? If you are a physiologist, you may be able to say, but that does not help you to open and close your hand any better than I do. I know how to do it, but I cannot put it into words. In the same way, you might say that God knows how he dreams this whole universe because he does it, but even he could not explain it. One might as well try to drink the Pacific Ocean with a fork. And when a Hindu gets enlightened and he recovers from the hallucination of being a skin-encapsulated ego, he finds out that central to his own self is the eternal self of the universe, and if you go up to him and say, "How do you do all this?" he is apt to say, "Well, just like you open and close your hand." Whenever questioners would go to Sri Ramana, the great Hindu sage who died years ago, they would say to him, "Master, was I living before in a previous incarnation, and if so, who was I?" And he would say to them, "Who is asking the question? Who are you?" What a spiritual teacher in both Hinduism and Buddhism does to awaken you, to get you over the hallucination of being the skin-encapsulated ego, is to annoy you in a certain way. He has a funny look in his eyes as if to say, "Come off it, Shiva, I know what you are up to, I know what you are doing." And you say, "What, me?" So he looks at you in this funny way until finally you get the feeling that he sees all the way through you; and that all your selfishness and evil, nasty thoughts are transparent to his gaze. Then you have to try and alter them. He suggests that you practice the control of the mind, that you become interiorly silent, and that you give up selfish desires of the skin-encapsulated self. Then you may have some success in quieting your mind and in concentrating. But after that, he will throw a curve at you, which is: Are you not still desiring not to desire? Why are you trying to be unselfish? Well, the answer is, "I want to be on the side of the big battalions. I think it is going to pay off better to be unselfish than to be selfish." Luther saw that, and St. Augustine saw it too. But there it is — he has begun to make you see the unreality and the hallucinatory quality of a separate self. Such a self is merely conventional reality, in the same sense as lines of latitude and longitude and the measurements of the clock; which is why one of the meanings of maya, illusion, is measurement. Things are measurements; they are units of thought, like inches are units of measurement. There are no *things* in physical nature. How many things are there in a thing? However many you want. A "thing" is a "think," a unit of thought; it is as much reality as you can catch hold of in one idea.

So when this realization of the hallucination of the separate self comes about, it comes about through discovering that your alleged separate self cannot do anything — it cannot improve itself either by doing something about it, or by doing nothing about it, and both ways are based on illusion. And this is what you have to do to get people out of their hallucinations — you make them act consistently on the suppositions of their hallucinations. The guru, whether Hindu or Buddhist, performs a *reductio ad absurdum* on the premise of the skin-encapsulated ego. So, what happens then? You might imagine from garbled accounts of Eastern mysticism that one thereupon disappears into an infinite sea of faintly mauve Jell-O, that you become so lost to the world, and so entranced that you forget your name, address, telephone number, and function in life. But nothing of the kind happens. The state of mystical illumination, although it may in its sudden onset be accompanied by a sensation of tremendous luminance and transparency, when you get used to it, it is just like everyday life. Here are the people that you formerly thought were separate individuals, and here is the "you" who you formerly thought was merely confronting these other people. When the great Dr. D. T. Suzuki was asked, "What is it like to be enlightened?" he said. "It is just like ordinary, everyday experience, except about two inches off the ground." You see, what is altered is not the way your senses perceive; what is altered is the way you think about it — your definitions of what you see, and your evaluation of it. When you do not cling to the world, and when you no longer have a hostile attitude toward it, you know the world is you. Taken from the point of view of biology, the behavior of a living organism cannot possibly be described without simultaneously describing the behavior of the environment. To describe organisms in environments is to describe a unified field of behavior called an "organism-environment." The environment does not push the organism around and the organism does not push the environment around. They are two aspects, or poles, of the same process.

This attitude toward nature — seeing the fundamental unity of the self that manifests it all — is not an attitude that, as missionaries are apt to suppose, denies the value of differentiation. You must understand the principle of what are called identical differences. Look at a coin: the head side is a different side from the tail side, and yet the two are inseparable. Take the operation of buying and selling. Selling is a separate operation from buying, but you cannot buy anything unless somebody is selling at the same time, and vice versa. This is what is meant by the underlying unity of opposites, what is called *advaita* or nonduality in Hinduism; and what the Chinese mean when they use the word *Tao* to designate the way of operation of the positive and negative principles, the yang and the yin. It is not a unity that annihilates differences, but a unity that is manifested by the very differentiations that we perceive. It is polar, like the two poles of one magnet. So when we say that Oriental monism is a point of view toward life that merges everything into a kind of sickening goo, this is terribly unfair. If you argue that this sort of doctrine, in which everybody is really the Godhead, destroys the possibility of love between individuals because you have to be definitively "other" in order to love, otherwise it is all self-love, then that argument collapses in view of the doctrine of the Trinity. If the three persons are one God, then they cannot love each other by the same argument. Hinduism simply uses the idea that is in the Christian Trinity, only it uses the idea of a multi-trinity. Instead of a three-in-One, it is a one-in-All.

Of course, the thorn in the flesh, when approaching a doctrine that seems to be monistic or pantheistic, is always — what about evil? Are we to make the ground of being responsible for evil? No, we do not want to do that because we want to keep God's skirts clean in spite of the fact that the Bible says: "I am the Lord, and there is none else; I form the light and create darkness; I make peace, and create evil. I the Lord do all these things." But who is it that sits at the left hand of God? (We know who sits at the right hand.) All talk about the one who sits on the left is hushed up because in court that is the side on which the district attorney sits. Of course, in the Book of Job, it is Satan who is the district attorney in the court of heaven. He is the prosecutor and faithful servant of the court. The whole problem is that it would be very bad indeed if God were the author of evil, and we were his victims. That is to say, if we keep the model of the king of the universe in which the creatures are all subjects of the king, then a God who is responsible for evil is being very unkind to the people. But in the Hindu theory, God is not another person. There are no victims of God. He is never anything but His own victim. You are responsible. If you want to stay in the state of illusion, stay in it. But you can always wake up.

CHAPTER SEVEN

RELIGION AND SEXUALITY

IN A VERY SPECIAL AND PECULIAR WAY, Western man is hung up on sex. The major reason for this is his religious background, which is quite unique among the religions of the world. I mean specifically Christianity, and in a secondary way, Judaism, insofar as Judaism in Europe and the United States is strongly influenced by Christianity. Of all religions in the world, Christianity is the one that is most uniquely preoccupied with sex, more so than tantric yoga or any kind of fertility cult that has ever existed on the face of the earth. There has never been a religion in which sexuality was so important.

In popular speech, when you say a person is living in sin, you know very well that you do not mean that they are engaged in a business to defraud the public by the sale of badly made bread, or setting up a check forgery business. People who are living in sin are those who have an irregular sexual partnership. In the same way, when you say something is immoral, it most often means something sexually irregular. When I was a boy in school, I remember we used to have a preacher who came to us once every year, and he always talked on the subject of drink, gambling, and immorality. The way he rolled it around his tongue, it was very clear what immorality was.

Most churches in America, England, and other parts of the Western world are, frankly, sexual regulation societies, and precious little else. They occasionally get excited about other moral issues, but really not very often. To prove this you only have to ask what people can be thrown out of church for. A person can live in envy, hatred, malice, and all uncharitableness and still be in perfectly good standing. But the moment anything about their sexual life becomes a little unusual, out they go, and that is about the only thing for which they can be removed.

For example, the Roman Catholic manuals of moral theology are technical books about sins of all kinds — what they are, how they are done, how grave they are — mostly for the advice of confessors. They are always arranged according to the Ten Commandments, and "Thou shalt not commit adultery" occupies two-thirds of the whole book, with all the details.

In a very special way, we have got sex on the brain, which is not exactly the right place for it. This needs examination, because it is not as simple as it looks. There are really two roots of the problem. One of them is the question of why, of all pleasures, religious people are particularly afraid of sexual pleasure. This is true not only of Christianity. Christianity emphasizes it in a certain way, but in Asian religions also, and especially in India, there is a prevailing view that if you want to attain real heights of spirituality, the one thing you must give up is sexuality, in the ordinary sense of genital sexual relationships. This reflects an attitude to the physical world, because it is through sexuality that we have, along with eating, our most fundamental relationship to materiality, to nature, to the physical universe. It is also the point at which we can become most attached to the body, to the physical organism and to material life. That is one reason why sexuality is problematic.

The other reason, which is more subtle, is that sexuality is something you cannot get rid of. Do what you may, life is sexual, in the sense that you are either male or female. There are various other gradations, but basically they are all forms of maleness and femaleness. And, of course, every one of you is the result of sexual intercourse. This sexual feature of life can be looked at in one of two ways. You can say, on the one hand, that all man's higher ideals, his spirituality and so forth, are simply repressed sexuality; on the other hand, you can say that human sexuality is a physical manifestation, a particular form of expression of what is spiritual, metaphysical, or divine. I hold to the latter view. I do not think that religion is repressed sexuality. Sexuality is just one of the many forms in which whatever all this is expresses itself. And sexuality is something you cannot get rid of. A way of life in which sexuality is in some way put down or repressed is nonetheless an expression of sexuality. If you realize this, then you come to a view of Christianity in which sex is a very special and unusual taboo.

And sex is taboo in Christianity; there is simply no getting around that. Up-to-date ministers today say sex is all right if you are married and you have a mature relationship with a member of the opposite sex. But if you read anything in Christian writings prior to approximately 1850, you will find that it is not all right at all. It is tolerated between married couples for the procreation of children, but on the whole it is best to do without. As St. Paul put it, it is better to marry than to burn in hell. In all the writings of the Church fathers from St. Paul himself to St. Ignatius Loyola to any of the great relatively modern leaders of Catholic spirituality, to Calvin and the great Protestants like John Knox, on the whole sex is sin and sex is dirt.

You can say very simply that this is very wrong, but I want to point out that there is another side to sexual prohibition. There is no way of making a hedge grow like pruning it. There is no way of making sex interesting like repressing it. Therefore, as a result of all these centuries of sexual repression and associating it with dirt, the West has developed a peculiar form of eroticism. That is an aspect of this whole problem that I do not think is really very profitable to explore, but I just want to mention in passing that the whole attitude of anti-sexuality in the Christian tradition is not as "anti" as it looks. It is simply a method of making sex prurient and exciting in a kind of dirty way. I suppose it is to be recommended to people who are not feeling very frisky and need to be pepped up.

The other side of the problem is much more interesting. That is, Why is pleasure a problem for human beings? We take sexual activity to be a supreme pleasure, and as a supreme involvement of oneself with the body and the physical world. Why should there be a problem with that? The answer is simply that the physical world is transient and impermanent; it falls apart. Bodies that were once strong, smooth, and lovely wither and become corrupt and turn at last into skeletons. If you cling to one of those bodies and it suddenly turns into a skeleton in your arms, as it will if you speed up your sense of time a little, you will feel cheated. There has been for centuries a lament about this. Life is so short, and all the beauties of this world fall apart. Therefore, if you are wise you do not set your heart on mortal beauty, you set your heart on spiritual values that are imperishable. Even Omar Khayyám says, "The worldly hope men set their hearts upon turns to ashes — or it prospers, and anon, like snow upon the desert's dusty face, lighting a little hour or two, is gone." So do not bet on that horse.

If you read any kind of spiritual literature, whether Christian, Buddhist, Hindu, or Taoist, you will find they all seem to emphasize the importance of detachment from the body, from the physical world, so that you won't be engulfed in the stream of impermanence. The idea is that, to the degree that you identify yourself with the body and with the pleasures of the body, you are simply identifying with something that will be sucked away in the course of transience. Therefore hold yourself aloof, advise many Hindus who practice yoga, and look on all sensory experiences as something out there, that you simply witness. You are to identify yourself with the eternal, spiritual, unchanging self — the witness of all that goes on — and are to be no more involved in the transitory than a mirror is involved in the things it reflects. Keep your mind pure and clean, free from dust, free from flaws, free from stain, and like a mirror just reflect everything that goes on without being attached.

It has always seemed to me that this attitude of essential detachment from the physical universe raises then the very serious question of why then have a physical universe at all? If God is in some way responsible for the existence of creation, and if this creation is basically a snare, why did He do it?

According to some theologians, the physical universe is looked on as a mistake, as a fall from the divine state, as if something went wrong in the heavenly domain, causing spirits, such as we are, in fact, to fall from their highest state and become involved with animal bodies. There is an ancient analogy, which runs right through to the present time, that your relationship to your body is that of a rider to a horse. St. Francis called his body Brother Ass. You are a rational soul in charge of an animal body, and therefore if you belong to the old school, you beat it into submission. Or if you are a Freudian you treat your horse not with a whip but kindly, with lumps of sugar; but it is still your horse. Even in Freud there is a very strong element of Puritanism. Read Philip Rieff's book

Freud: The Mind of the Moralist. In it he shows that Freud basically thought that sex was something degrading, though nevertheless unavoidable and terribly necessary, which could not be swept aside but had to be dealt with. But there is still in this the heritage of thinking of ourselves as divided, of the ego as the rational soul of spiritual origin and the physical body as the animal component. Therefore, in this heritage, all spiritual success requires the spiritualization of the animal component, the sublimation of its dirty and strange urges. I suppose the ideal sexual relationship of such persons would be held on an operating table under disinfectant sprays.

Of course, it is true that the physical world and its beauty is transient. We are all falling apart in some way or other, especially after we pass the peak of youth. But this has never struck me as something to gripe about. That the physical world is transient seems to be part of its splendor. I can imagine nothing more awful than attaining the age of thirty and suddenly being frozen in that age for always. You would become a kind of animated waxwork; people with a physical permanence like that would feel like plastic. As a matter of fact, that is what is going to be done about us by technology in order to provide perpetual youth. All the parts of our bodies that decay and fold up are going to be replaced by very skillfully manufactured plastic parts, so that in the end we will be entirely made of very sophisticated plastic. Everybody will feel like plastic, and everybody will be utterly bored with each other, because the very fact that the world is always decaying and falling away is the source of its very vitality. Vitality is change. Life is death; it is always falling apart.

There are certain supreme moments when, in the body, we attain superb vitality. It is just like when an orchestra is playing and the conductor wants a certain group of violinists to come in at a certain moment, and they do. That is the whole art of life, to do it at the right time. In the same way, when it comes to love, sexuality, or, equally, all the pleasures of gastronomy, timing is of the essence. You have them for a moment, and then they are gone, but that is not something that one should look on with regret. It is regrettable only if you don't know how to accept it when its moment arrives.

This is really the essence of what I want to talk about, because to be detached from the world, in the sense that Buddhists and Taoists and Hindus often talk about detachment, does not mean to be nonparticipative. You can have a very rich and full sexual life, and yet all the time be detached. By that I do not mean that you just go through it mechanically and have your thoughts elsewhere. I mean a complete participation, but still detached. The difference between the two attitudes is this: On the one hand, there is a way of being so anxious about physical pleasure, so afraid that you won't make it, that you grab it too hard and destroy it completely. After every failed attempt to get it you feel disappointed and empty; you feel something was lost, and so you have to keep repeating, repeating, repeating. This is the hang-up. This is what is meant by attachment to this world, in the negative sense of the word. Pleasure in its fullness cannot be experienced when one is grasping it.

I knew a little girl to whom someone gave a bunny rabbit. She was so delighted with it and so afraid of losing it that taking it home in the car she squeezed it to death. Lots of parents do that to their children, and to each other. They hold on too hard, and so take the life out of this transient, beautifully fragile thing that life is. To have life and its pleasure you must, at the same time, let go of it. Then you can feel perfectly free to have that pleasure in the most gutsy, rollicking, earthshaking, lip-licking way, with one's whole being taken over by a kind of undulative, convulsive ripple, like the very pulse of life itself. But, this can happen only if you let go, if you are willing to be abandoned.

87

That word, *abandoned*, is funny. We speak of people who are dissolute as being abandoned, but abandoned is also a characteristic of a saint. A great spiritual book by a Jesuit father is called *Abandonment to Divine Providence*. There are people who just are not hung up. They are those who, out of their spirituality, do not cling to any property. They do not carry burdens around. They are free, and just that sort of let-go-ness is quite essential for the enjoyment of any kind of pleasure at all, and particularly sexual pleasure.

I do not know how typical this would be of children brought up in a religious environment in the United States, but my experience as a boy in school in England was quite fascinating. When a child is baptized and is too young to know anything about its meaning, its godfather and godmother are the sponsors. When you are about to enter into puberty, however, and are confirmed, you yourself undertake your own baptismal vows. In confirmation into the Church of England, which is Episcopalian in this country, confirmation is preceded by instruction. In England this instruction consisted very largely of lessons in Church history, because the British approach to religion is peculiarly archeological, based on the great Christian saints and heroes of the past. It is really quite interesting, because it somehow associates you with the tradition of King Arthur and the Knights of the Round Table, and all that sort of thing. But the time comes when every candidate for confirmation has a private talk with the school chaplain. In every process of initiation into mysteries, from time immemorial, there has been the passing on of a secret. So there is a certain anticipation about this very private communication, because you would think that, being initiated into a religion, the secret would consist of some marvelous information about the nature of God or the fundamental reason for being. But it is not so. Instead, the initiatory secret talk was a serious lecture on the evils of masturbation. What these evils were was not clearly specified, but it was vaguely hinted that ghastly diseases would result. So, in a perverse sort of way, we candidates for confirmation used to enjoy tormenting ourselves with imagining what kind of terrible diseases — venereal disease, epilepsy, tuberculosis, or the great Siberian itch — would result from this practice.

The extraordinary thing is that the chaplain who gave these lectures had, in his own upbringing, been given the same lecture by other chaplains, and I imagine this went back some distance in history. Of course they all knew perfectly well that one of the characteristic behavior patterns of adolescence is ritual defiance of authority. You have to make some protest against authority, and in doing so you are in league with all your contemporaries, your peer group. Nobody would dream of giving anybody else away, because then he would be a tattletale, a skunk, and definitely not one of the boys. Therefore, obviously, masturbation provided the ideal outlet for this ritual defiance because it was fun, it was also an assertion of masculinity, and it was very, very wicked.

In the religious background of the Western world, we have mainly two traditions, one is Semitic, and the other is Greek. So far as the Semitic tradition is concerned, the material world and sexuality are definitely good things. Both Jews and Muslims think that God's creation of beautiful women was a grand idea. *The Perfumed Garden*, the Arabic book that is the Islamic version of the *Kama Sutra*, opens with a prayer to Allah that is a very full, detailed thanksgiving for the loveliness of women, with which Allah has blessed mankind. In the Book of Proverbs, we are enjoined to enjoy our wives while they are young. But even so, on the whole it is the Semitic belief that sexuality is justified solely for purposes of reproduction. This is what makes it good in the eyes of God, and that is the limitation put on it. Sexual energy should not really be wasted for other purposes.

In contrast to this we have a Greek tradition that was strongly influenced by a dualistic view of the universe, in which material existence is conceived of as a trap, a fall into turgid, clogging matter that is antagonistic to the lightness and freedom of the spirit. Therefore, for certain kinds of Greek religions — among which we must name the Orphic Mysteries, the Neoplatonic point of view, and the late agnostic points of view — being saved means being delivered from material existence into a purely spiritual state. From this point of view, sexual involvement is the very archetype of material environment — *martyr*, *mother*, *mater*, and *matter* are really the same word. So the love of woman is the great snare. This is, incidentally, a doctrine invented by men. It goes back to the words of Adam, "The woman that thou gavest me, she tempted me, and I did eat."

In the development of Christian theology, from approximately the time of St. Paul through the beginning of the Renaissance, it was universally held that sex was a bad thing. Read St. Augustine; he said that in the Garden of Eden before the Fall, reproduction took place in just the same place and with just the same lack of excitement as one excretes, or passes water. There was no shameful excitation of the sexual parts. The whole attitude of the Church fathers in those centuries was that the virgin state was immensely superior spiritually to the marriage state, and that sexual relationships were excusable only within the bonds of marriage and for the sole purpose of reproduction. The manuals and moral penitentiaries of the theologians of the Middle Ages list all sorts of penances that must be said, even by married couples who performed sexual intercourse on the night before attending mass or receiving Holy Communion. Of course, sex must be avoided completely on certain great church festivals. Although in theory marriage is a sacrament that somehow blesses this peculiar relationship, there is a definite attitude that even within that sacrament sex is still dirty and not very nice.

You must realize, also, that in those days the institution of marriage was not what it is today. Marriage at the time of the rise of Christianity was a social institution for creating alliances between families. You did not marry the person of your choice except under the most unusual circumstances. You married the girl your family picked out for you, and they thought it over carefully from its political point of view, as well as from the point of view of eugenics, and economics. You married this girl even though you were not necessarily in love with her, and it was perfectly well understood in the secular world that on the side you had other arrangements. If you could afford them, you had concubines or even second and third and fourth wives. There was somewhat more freedom of choice about those subsidiary wives, but the first one was definitely a family arrangement. That is the context of the Church's saying that only that woman whose marriage has been arranged by paternal authority should be your bedfellow.

The idea of romantic love does not arrive in connection with marriage until the troubadour cults of Provence in southern France in the late Middle Ages. Then begins the idealization of woman as the inspiring goddess, and also the idea of the knight-errant. Dante's Beatrice is the inspiring woman who leads him to heaven. Historians today are not agreed as to whether the ladyloves of the chivalrous knights were in fact their mistresses or were simply idealized woman, but the influence of the cult of romantic love on the West was profound. And it brought about a weird combination of ideas: first, the notion of the married state being the only licit relationship in which sexual play might be carried on, and second, the notion that the girl you marry should be the one with whom you have fallen in love. Two more ill-adjusted ideas could hardly be put together, because naturally when you love someone very much indeed, in your enthusiasm to become involved you say things that are hardly logical, or rational. You may stand up before an altar and say, "My darling, my sweetheart, my perfect pet, I adore you so much that I will live with you forever and ever, until death do us part." Although that is the way you feel at the time, this level of enthusiasm may not last. In a rather similar mood, ancient people would hail their kings and say, "O King, live forever." Obviously this was not meant literally; they were just wishing him a long life.

The trouble was that when that kind of extravagant poetic expression fell into the hands of people like Augustine, who were rather influenced by Roman literalists, they wrote it into the law books. Thereby an amazing situation came about, and we still have not fully explored its subtlety. Consider certain periods when this attitude of prudery toward sexuality was in ascendancy. Nearest to our time is the bourgeois revolution in Victorian England and the United States. *Victorian* is usually a term of invective indicating extreme monogamy and a definite disgust for all things sexual. Yet, when really examining the history of the Victorian period, we find that it was an extremely lascivious epoch. One has only to look at the lushness of Victorian furniture to realize that chairs were disguised women; even the way piano legs were shaped reflects this influence.

People like Freud and Havelock Ellis made a certain mistake. They said the Church, and religion in general, was nothing but a form of sublimated sex. They said, "For whatever curious reasons these people suppressed sex, and therefore it became a very powerful force for them." To understand this you must remember that they used a hydraulic analogy of human psychology. They likened it to a river — if you damned it up, it could burst the dam. It does not actually follow that human psychology is akin to hydraulics, but this is the metaphor Ellis and Freud used. They said, "The Church has repressed sex, but if you look at its symbolism you will see that it is actually a robust expression of sexuality. Everything is reduced to libido as the fundamental reality," they said. The Church replied to this by saying, "It is nothing of the kind. Reducing the Church to repressed sex is just a way of attacking holy things, and on the contrary, we would say that people who are fascinated with sex and make it their god are repressing religion."

The problem in this debate is that everybody has missed the boat. The Church should have said to Freud, "Thank you very much. Yes indeed, our symbolism is sexual. The steeples of our churches, the vesicle-shaped windows and heraldic shields on which we put our images of the crucifix or the Virgin Mother of God, these are all quite plainly sexual. However, the sexual form reveals the mysteries of the universe. Sex is not mere sex. It is a holy thing, and one of our most marvelous revelations of the divine." But the Church just could not say that.

When one looks at Tibetan Buddhist iconography and images, or Hindu temples, one finds things that Europeans and Americans have never been able to understand. Here are images of buddhas and the gods engaged in amazing diversions with their female counterparts. Everybody thinks that these are dirty sculptures, but they are nothing of the kind. They reveal to the people who look at them that the play of man and woman is, on the level of biology, a reflection of the fundamental play of the cosmos. The positive and negative principles, the light and the dark, the mental and the material, all play together. The purpose of sexual play is not merely the utilitarian function of reproducing the species, as it seems to be among animals to a very large extent. What peculiarly distinguishes human sexuality is that it brings the partners closer and closer to each other in an intense state of united feeling. In other words, it is a sacrament, the outward and visible sign of an inward and spiritual grace, that brings about love. So, as that union seems to be peculiar to human beings, it is perfect nonsense to degrade human sexuality by saying it should only be carried on in the way that animals must, because they have not yet evolved to the place where sex is a sacramental expression of love. Falling in love, while considered by practical people to be a sort of madness, is actually the same sort of thing as the mystical vision, or grace. In this light we see people in their divine aspect. When the song says, "Every little breeze whispers Louise," it is singing that there is a sort of extraordinary state of mystical intoxication in which every woman becomes a goddess and, likewise, every man becomes a god.

What happened, however, as a result of this conflict between proponents of religion and the proponents of scientific naturalism was mutual name-calling. They have never come together because neither the Church nor the opponents of the Church has clearly understood that sexuality and all that goes with it is a triggering forth, on the level of biology, of what the whole universe is about — and that is ecstatic play. As a result, there has been a kind of compromise. In ecclesiastical circles, sex is being damned with faint praise. People are saying, "After all, sex was made by God, and perhaps it is something more than reproduction, it may bring about the cementing of the marriage ties between husband and wife," but in practice it remains the frightening taboo.

At the same time, the opposition to Christian prudery always goes overboard in the direction of total license. So we have a contest between the people who want skirt hems down to the floor and the people who want them pulled up over the head, and it seems you have to draw the line somewhere. The play between these forces is over the question of where we shall draw the line, and that is very exciting play, providing neither side wins. Imagine what it would be like if the libertines won and they took over the Church on Wednesday evenings so the young Presbyterian group could meet for prayer through sex. Every child would go to the school physician for a course in hygienics, and they would have classes and plastic models, and then the children would do it in class in a very hygienic atmosphere. Imagine how boring it would all become in this setting. So the people who say that modesty is important are saying something that is quite right. They must not be allowed to prevail, but they must not be obliterated either. In life the balance of oppositions works that way.

To use an entirely different analogy, take a given biological group, a species we will call A. It has a natural enemy, B. One day A gets furious at its natural enemy B and says, "Let us obliterate B." They gather their forces and knock out their enemy. After a while, they begin to get weak and overpopulated. There is nobody around to eat up their surplus members, and they do not have to keep their muscles strong to defend against an enemy. They begin to fall apart because they have destroyed their enemy, and they remember that what they should do is cultivate the enemy. That is the real meaning of "Love your enemy." There is such a thing as a beloved enemy. If the flies and the spiders did not have each other, there would be either too many spiders or too many flies. These balances maintain the course of nature.

It is exactly the same with the libertines and the prudes. They need each other. If you have a prudish father and mother, you should be very grateful to them for having made sex so interesting. Still, every generation must react to the one before it, and this keeps the tension going. It is by this play of opposites that we know separation and seek the love that makes the world go round.

PART THREE

1965–1967

1965-1987

CHAPTER EIGHT

FROM TIME TO ETERNITY

WHEN ST. AUGUSTINE OF HIPPO was asked, "What is time?" he replied, "I know what it is, but when you ask me, I don't." Amusingly enough, he is the man most responsible for the commonsensical idea of time that prevails in the West.

The Greeks and East Indians thought of time as a circular process. Anyone looking at a watch will obviously see that time goes around. But the Hebrews and the Christians thought of time as something that goes in a straight line. And that is a powerful idea, which influences everybody living in the West today.

We all have our various mythologies. When I use the word *mythology*, or *myth*, I don't mean something that is false. I mean an idea or image by which people make sense of the world.

The Western myth, under which our common sense has been nurtured over many centuries, is that the world began in the year 4000 B.C. This myth is presented in the King James Bible, which descended from heaven with an angel in the year 1611. According to this myth, the Lord God naturally had existed forever and ever and ever, through endless time. The world was created, and then it fell apart. And so, in the middle of time, the second person of the Trinity incarnated himself in the form of Jesus Christ in order to save mankind and establish the true Church. Sometime in the future, time will come to an end. There will be a day that will be the Last Day, in which the second person of the Trinity — God the Son — will appear again in glory with his legions of angels. And the Last Judgment will be held. And those who are saved will live forever and ever in contemplation of the vision of the Blessed Trinity. And those who did not behave themselves will squirm forever in hell.

Time, according to this presentation, is unidirectional. Each event happens once, and it can never be repeated. According to St. Augustine, when God the Son came into this world, he sacrificed himself for the remission of all sins. That was an event that could happen once and only once.

I don't know why he thought that, but he sure did think it. And so we have the idea that time is a unique story that had a definite beginning and is going to have a definite end, and that's that. Most Westerners do not believe in this story anymore, although many of them think that they ought to believe in it. But even though they don't believe in it, they still retain from it a way of thinking, a linear view of time, that says that we are going down a one-way road. We will never again go back over the course that we have followed. And we hope, as we go on, that in time, things will get progressively better and better.

This version of time differs in a very strange and fascinating way from the view of time held by most other people in the world. Take the Hindu view of time. The Hindus are not so small-minded and provincial as to believe that the world was created as recently as 4000 B.C. They calculate the ages of the universe in units of

4,320,000 years. That is their basic counting unit, and it is called a *kalpa*. And so, their understanding of the world is quite different from ours.

We in the West think of the world as an artifact, made by a grand technician, the Creator. But the Hindus do not think that the world was created at all. They look upon it as a drama — not as having been created, but as being acted. They see God as the supreme actor, or as what is called the cosmic self, playing all the different parts simultaneously. In other words, you and the birds and bees and flowers and rocks and stars are all an act put on by God, who is pretending to be all these things, through the many eternities, in order to amuse himself. He is pretending that he is all of us. And this is not, after all, such an unreasonable idea. If I were to ask you to consider what you would do if you were God, you might find that being omniscient, all-powerful, and eternal would eventually become extremely boring. Eventually you would want a surprise.

What are we trying to do with our technology? We are trying to control the world. We are trying to become all-powerful and omniscient. Imagine the ultimate fulfillment of that desire. When we are in control of everything and we have great panels of push buttons whereby the slightest touch fulfills every wish, what will we want then? We will eventually want to arrange to have a special, red button marked "surprise" built into the panel. Touch that button and what happens? We will suddenly disappear from our normal consciousness and find ourselves in a situation very much like the one we are now in, where we feel ourselves to be a little bit out of control, subject to surprises, and subject to the whims of an unpredictable universe.

The Hindus figure that God presses the surprise button every so often. That is to say, for a period of 4,320,000 years, God knows who He is. And then He gets bored with that and forgets who He is for an equal period of 4,320,000 years. He goes to sleep and has a dream, and this dream is called the *Manvantara*. The period in which He wakes up and is not dreaming is called the *Pralaya*, a state of total bliss. But when He has a dream, He manifests the world.

This manifestation of the world is divided into four ages. They are named after the four throws in the Indian game of dice. The first throw is *krita*, which is the throw of four, the perfect throw. The *Krita-yuga*, or first age, lasts a very long time.

In this period of the manifestation of the world, everything is absolutely delightful. It would be the same, for example, if you had the privilege of dreaming any dream you wanted to dream when you went to sleep at night. For at least a month you would live out all your wishes in your dreams. You would have banquets and music and everything that you ever thought you wanted.

But then, after a few weeks of this, you would say, "Well, this is getting a little dull. Let's have an adventure. Let's get into trouble." It is all right to get into trouble because you know you are going to wake up at the end of it. So you could fight dragons and rescue princesses, and all that sort of thing.

After a while, when that got boring, you could get more and more far out. You could arrange to forget that you were dreaming. You would believe you really were involved in danger, and what a surprise it would be when you woke up. And then, one of those nights, when you were dreaming any dream you wanted to dream, you would even find yourself sitting where you are right now, with all your special problems and hang-ups and reading and involvement, reading these words. How do you know that that is not what is happening?

So then, after the Krita-yuga in which everything is perfect, there comes a somewhat shorter epoch called the *Treta-yuga*, named after the throw of three in the Hindu game of dice. And in the Treta-yuga, things are a little bit less secure.

When that epoch comes to an end, there comes the third: a shorter period called the *Dvapara-yuga* — named after *dva*, the throw of two. In this period, the forces of good and evil are equally balanced.

When that era comes to an end, there follows a still shorter period called the *Kali-yuga*. *Kali* means the throw of one, or the worst throw. And in this period, the forces of negation and destruction are finally triumphant.

The Kali-yuga is supposed to have started shortly before 3000 B.C. We have another five thousand years of it to go. In this period, everything falls apart, and things get worse and worse and worse, until finally, at the end, the Lord himself appears in the disguise of Kali, the destroyer. Kali is black-bodied, has four arms, and wears a necklace of skulls. In one hand, he holds a bloody sword. A second hand holds a severed head by the hair. A third hand is open, fingers extended forward in the boon-giving gesture. The fourth hand is also open, fingers pointing up, palm exposed in the gesture that means don't be afraid, everything is just a big act. Thereupon the entire cosmos is destroyed in fire, and in every soul the Lord wakes up again and discovers who He is, and abides for a Pralaya of 4,320,000 years in a state of total bliss.

This sequence of eras repeats forever. It is the in-breathing and out-breathing of Brahma, the supreme self. And they add up into years of Brahma, each one of which is three hundred and sixty kalpas. And these in turn add up again into centuries, and it goes on and on and on. But it never gets boring because every time the new Manvantara starts, the Lord God forgets everything that happened before and becomes completely absorbed in the act, just as you did when you were born and you opened your eyes on the world for what you thought was the first time. All the world was strange and wonderful. You saw it with the clear eyes of a child.

Of course, as you get older, you get more used to things. You have seen the sun again and again, and you think it is just the same old sun. You have seen the trees until you regard them as the same old trees. And finally, you begin to get bored and you start to fall apart and disintegrate until you die because you have had enough of it. But then after you die, another baby is born who is of course you, because every baby calls itself I and sees the whole thing from a new point of view again, and is perfectly thrilled. And so in this way, arranged wonderfully, so that there is never any absolutely intolerable boredom, the time goes on and on and on and around and around and around.

This Hindu myth is one of the great myths of time in the world. And we, in our day and age, need to consider this myth very seriously. As a highly technological civilization with enormous power over nature, we really need to consider time. Therefore, let me ask again the question that was asked of St. Augustine: "What is time?" I am not going to give you his answer. I know what time is, and when you ask me I will tell you. Time is a measure of energy, a measure of motion.

We have agreed internationally on the speed of the clock. So I want you to think about clocks and watches for a moment. We are, of course, slaves to them. And you will notice that your watch has a circular face, and that it is calibrated. Each minute or second is marked by a hairline, made as narrow as possible, while yet remaining visible. When we think of what we mean by the word *now*, we think of the shortest possible instant that is here and then gone immediately, because that thought corresponds with the image of the hairline calibrations on a watch.

As a result, we are a people who feel that we don't have any present, because we believe that the present is always instantly vanishing. This is the problem of Goethe's Faust. He attains his great moment and says to it, "Oh still delay, thou art so fair." But the moment never stays. It is always disappearing into the past.

Therefore we have the sensation that our lives are constantly flowing away from us. And so we have a sense of urgency: Time is not to waste; time is money. And so, because of the tyranny of clocks, we feel that we have a past, and that we know who we were in the past — nobody can ever tell you who they *are*; they can only tell you who they *were* — and we believe we also have a future. And that belief is terribly important, because we have a naive hope that the future is somehow going to supply us with everything we're looking for.

You see, if you live in a present that is so short that it is not really there at all, you will always feel vaguely frustrated. When you ask a person, "What did you do yesterday?" he will give you a historical account of a sequence of events. He will say, "I woke up at about seven o'clock in the morning. I got up and made myself some coffee, and then I brushed my teeth and took a shower, got dressed, had some breakfast, and went down to the office." He gives you a historical outline of a course of events. And people really think that is what they did.

But actually that is only a very skeletal account of what they did. People live a much richer life than that, but they don't notice it. They only pay attention to a very small part of the information received through their five senses. They forget that when they got up in the morning and made some coffee, their eyes slid across the birds outside their window. They forget about the light on the leaves of the tree, and that their nose played games with the scent of the coffee. They forget because they weren't aware of it, because they were in a hurry. They were engaged in consuming that coffee as fast as possible so that they could get to their office to do something they thought was terribly important.

And maybe it was, in a certain way; it made money. But, because they were so absorbed with the future, they had no use for the money they made. They couldn't enjoy it. Maybe they invested it so that they could have a future in which something finally might happen to them, the something that they were looking for all along. But of course, it never will happen to them, because tomorrow never comes. The truth of the matter is that there is no such thing as time. Time is a hallucination. There is only today. There never will be anything except today. And if you do not know how to live today, you are demented.

This is the great problem of Western civilization, of all civilizations. Civilization is a very complex system in which we use symbols — words, numbers, figures, and concepts — to represent the real world of nature. We use money to represent wealth. We use the clock to represent time. We use yards and inches to represent space. These are very useful measures. But you can always have too much of a good thing. You can easily confuse the measurement with what you are measuring, such as confusing money with wealth. It is like confusing the menu with dinner. You can become so enchanted with the symbols that you entirely confuse them with the reality. This is the disease from which almost all civilized people are suffering. We are, therefore, in the position of eating the menu instead of the dinner, of living in a world of words and symbols. This causes us to relate badly to our material surroundings.

The United States of America, as the most progressive country of the West, is the great example of this. We are a people who believe ourselves to be the great materialists, and we are slightly ashamed of it. But this is an absolutely undeserved reputation. A materialist is a person who loves material and therefore reveres it, respects it, and enjoys it. We don't do that. We are a people who hate material. We're devoting ourselves to the abolition of its limitations. We want to abolish the limits of time and space. We want to get rid of space. We call it the conquest of space. We want to be able to get from San Francisco to New York in nothing flat. And we are arranging to do just that. We do not realize what the result of doing that will be: San Francisco and New York will become the same place, and then it will not be worth going from one to another.

When you want to go on vacation, you want to go someplace that's different. You might think of Hawaii, where you imagine sandy beaches, the lovely blue ocean, and coral reefs. But tourists are increasingly asking of such a place, "Has it been spoiled yet?" By this they mean, "Is it exactly like Dallas yet?" And the answer is, "Yes." The faster you can get from Dallas to Honolulu, the faster Honolulu is becoming the same place as Dallas and the less reason there is to make the trip. Tokyo has become the same place as Los Angeles. As you go faster and faster from place to place on the earth, they are all becoming the same place. That is the result of abolishing the limitations of time and space.

We are in a hurry about too many things. Going back to my account of someone's day: The person got up in the morning and made some coffee, and I suppose it was instant coffee, because that person was in too much of a hurry to be concerned with the preparation of a beautiful cup of coffee. Instant coffee is a punishment for people who are in too much of a hurry.

This is true of everything that's instant. There is something phony and fake about it. Where were you rushing into the future? What did you think the future was going to bring you? Actually, you don't know. I've always thought it an excellent idea to assign to freshmen in college the task of writing an essay on what they would like heaven to be. In other words, to make them think about what they really want in that abstraction the future. Because the truth of the matter is this — as I have already intimated — there is no such thing as the future. Time is an abstraction. So is money, for that matter. So are inches.

Think about the Great Depression. One day everything was going along fine — everybody was pretty wealthy and had plenty to eat — and the next day, suddenly, everybody was in poverty. What happened? Had the farms disappeared? Had the cows vanished into thin air? Had the fish of the sea ceased to exist? Had human beings lost their energy, their skills, and their brains? No. This is what happened: On the morning after the beginning of the Depression, a carpenter came to work, and the foreman said to him. "Sorry, chum, you can't work today. There ain't no inches."

The carpenter said, "What do you mean, there ain't no inches?"

"Yeah," the foreman said. "We got lumber, we got metal, but we ain't got no inches."

"You're crazy," the carpenter said.

And the foreman replied, "The trouble with you is you don't understand business."

What happened in the Great Depression was that human beings confused money with wealth. And they didn't realize that money is a measure of wealth, in exactly the same way that inches are a measure of length. They think it is something that is valuable in and of itself. And as a result of that they get into unbelievable trouble.

In the same way, time is nothing but an abstract measure of motion. And we keep counting time. We have the sensation that time is running out, and we bug ourselves with this. Suppose you are working. Are you watching the clock? If you are, what are you waiting for? Time off. Five o'clock. You can go home and have fun. What are you going to do when you get home? Have fun? Or are you going to watch TV — which is an electronic reproduction of life that doesn't even smell of anything — and eat a TV dinner — which is a kind of warmed-over airline nastiness — until you just get tired and have to go to sleep?

This is our problem, you see. We are not alive. We are not awake. We are not living in the present. Take education. What a hoax. As a child, you are sent to nursery school. In nursery school, they say you are getting ready to go on to kindergarten. And then first grade is coming up and second grade and third grade. They say you are gradually climbing the ladder, making progress. And then, when you get to the end of grade school, they say, "You've been getting ready for high school." And then in high school, they tell you you're getting ready for college. And in college you're getting ready to go out into the business world with your suit and your diploma. And you go to your first sales meeting, and they say, "Now get out there and sell this stuff." They say you'll be going on up the ladder in business if you sell it, and maybe you'll get a promotion. And you sell it, and they up your quota. And then, finally at about the age of forty-five, you wake up one morning as vice president of the firm, and you say to yourself, "I've arrived. But I've been cheated. Something is missing. I no longer have a future." "Wrong," says the insurance salesman. "I have a future for you. This policy will enable you to retire in comfort at sixty-five, and now you can look forward to that." And you're delighted. You buy the policy, and at sixty-five, you retire, thinking that this is the attainment of the goal of life. Except that now you have prostate trouble, false teeth, and wrinkled skin. And you're a materialist. You're a phantom. You are an abstraction. You are nowhere, because you were never told, and you never realized, that eternity is now. There is no time.

What will you do then? Can you recover the pop of a champagne cork that popped last night? Can you hand me a copy of tomorrow's *Dallas Morning Herald*? It just isn't there. There is not time. Time is a fantasy. It is a useful fantasy, just as the lines of latitude and longitude are. But they aren't real lines. You are never going to tie up a package with the equator. It and time are the same; they're abstractions. Time is a convenience. It allows us to arrange to meet each other at the corner of Main and First at four o'clock. Great. But let us not be fooled by convenience. It is not real.

People who live in the present have absolutely no use for making plans. People who believe in time and who believe that they are living for their future make plenty of plans. But when the plans mature, the people are not there to enjoy them. They are busy planning something else. And they are like donkeys running after carrots that are hanging in front of their faces from sticks attached to their own collars. They are never here. They never get there. They are never alive. They are perpetually frustrated. And therefore they are always thinking. The future is the thing with them. Someday it is going to happen, they think. And because it never does, they are frantic. They want more time, more time, please, more time. They are terrified of death, because death stops the future. And so they never get there, wherever *there* is. There is always somewhere else, around the corner.

Please, wake up.

I am not saying that you should be improvident, that you shouldn't have an insurance policy, that you shouldn't be concerned about how you are going to send your children to college. Except that there is no point in sending your children to college and providing for their future if you don't know how to live in the present, because all you will do is teach your children how not to live in the present. You will end up dragging yourself through life for the alleged benefit of your own children, who will in turn drag out their lives in a boring way for the alleged benefit of their children. Everybody is looking after everybody else so beautifully that nobody has any fun at all. We say of a person who is insane that he is not all here. Not being all here is our collective disease.

In the beginning of the regime of communism in Russia, they had five-year plans, and everything was going to be great at the end of the five years, except that when they got to the end, they had to make another five-year plan. They were making human beings into a floor on which the next generation would dance. But, of course, the next generation wouldn't be able to dance; it would have to become the floor for the generation after that. And so on. Each generation holds up the floor above it, forever and ever, and nobody ever dances.

But you see, the philosophy of the communists and our philosophy are exactly the same. In fact, our system is their system. And increasingly, we and they are becoming more and more alike, because of our misperception of the reality of time. We are obsessed with time. It is always coming. Mao Tse-tung can say to all the Chinese, "Live a great boring life and wear the same clothes and carry around a little red book and one day, perhaps, everything will be great."

And we are in exactly the same situation. We are the richest people in the world, and most of our businessmen go around in dark suits looking like undertakers. We eat Wonder Bread, which is Styrofoam injected with some chemicals that are supposed to be nutritious. We do not even know how to eat. In other words, we live in the abstract, not in the concrete. We work for money, not for wealth. We look forward to the future and do not know how to enjoy today. And we are destroying our environment. We are Los Angelizing the world, instead of civilizing it. We are turning the air into gas fumes and the water into poison. We are tearing the vegetation off the face of the hills. And for what? To print newspapers.

In our colleges, we value the record of what has happened more than we value what is happening. The records in the registrar's office are kept in safes under lock and key, but not the books in the library. What you do is, of course, much more important than what you did. We don't understand this. We go out on a picnic, and somebody says, "We are having a lovely time. What a pity somebody didn't bring a camera." People go on tours with wretched little boxes around their necks, and instead of being in the scene, whatever it is, they go click, click, click with those little boxes so that when they get home they can show photographs to their friends and say, "See what happened. Of course I wasn't really there, I was just photographing it."

When the record becomes more important than the event, we are really up the creek with no paddle. So the most serious need of civilization is to come to now. Think of all the trouble we would save. Think of how peaceful things would become. We would not be interfering with everybody. We would not be doing everybody else good, like the general who destroyed a village in Vietnam for its own safety. That is the explanation he gave. "Kindly let me help you or you will drown," said the monkey, putting the fish safely up a tree.

Now is the meaning of eternal life. Jesus said, "Before Abraham was, I am." He didn't say, "I was." He said, "I am." And to come to this, to know that you are and there is no time except the present, is to suddenly attain a sense of reality.

The aim of education ought to be to teach people to live in the present, to be all here. Instead, our educational system is pretty abstract. It neglects the absolute fundamentals of life and instead teaches us to be bureaucrats, bank clerks, accountants, and insurance salesmen. It entirely neglects our relationships to the material world of which there are five: farming, cooking, clothing, housing, and lovemaking. These are grossly overlooked. And so it becomes possible for the Congress of the United States to pass a law making it a grave penalty for anyone to burn the flag. Yet those same Congressmen, by acts of commission or omission, are responsible for burning up what the flag stands for and for the erosion of the natural resources of this land. Although they say they love their country, they don't. Their country is a reality. They love their flag, which is an abstraction. So I think it is time to get back to reality, to get back from time to eternity, to get back to the eternal now, which is what we have, always have had, and indeed always will have.

CHAPTER NINE

TAOIST WAYS

IN THE INITIAL STAGES OF ZEN TRAINING, the master will discourage thinking.

Although you may come to him with a lot of ideas, your difficulty is not going to be solved by your ideas. It is not going to be solved by talk and intellectualization, and so they are not encouraged. Intellectualization creates a gap or lack of rapport between you and your life. You may think about things so much that you get into the state where you are eating the menu instead of the dinner, where you value money more than wealth, and are generally confusing the map with the territory. So what the master wants to do is get you to become part of the landscape, and to get you into relationship with what is as distinct from ideas about what is. This is a very important preliminary discipline, but later on you may also realize that the process of thinking is also what is, that thoughts in their own domain are as real as rocks, and words have their own reality as much as sky and water. Thoughts about things are in their own turn things, and lead you eventually to the point where you can intellectualize and think in an immediate way.

The philosophy of Tao sees man as a part of nature rather than dominating it. There are several well-known Chinese landscape paintings with the title *Poet Drinking by Moonlight*. When you look at any one of them, at first you see a vast landscape. Only after searching very thoroughly, almost with a magnifying glass, do you finally find the poet tucked away in a corner of the painting drinking wine. If, however, the subject *Poet Drinking by Moonlight* were painted by a Western painter, the poet would be the central figure, dominating the whole picture, and the landscape a mere backdrop. Of course some Chinese painters specialized in family portraits and painted very formal paintings of ancestors on their thrones, but the Taoist and Zen-inspired painters portrayed man as an integral part of nature.

Man is something in nature, just as everything else is, including mountains and streams, trees, flowers, and birds. He is not commissioned by some sort of supernatural being to farm or dominate nature. The Taoists see nature as a self-regulating, self-governing, and indeed, democratic organism — a totality. It all goes together, and this totality is the Tao.

When we speak in Taoism of following the course of nature, or following the way, what we mean is doing things in accord with the grain. This does not mean we do not cut wood, but that when we cut wood we cut along the grain, where the wood cuts most easily. In relationships with other people, we try to interact along the lines that are the most genial. This is the great, fundamental principal called *wu wei*, or "not forcing." Wu wei is often translated as "not doing," "not acting," or "not interfering," but "not forcing" seems to me to hit the nail on the head. Never force a lock because you will bend the key or break the lock. Instead jiggle the key until it turns. Wu wei means always acting in accord with the pattern of things as they are.

When we follow the principle of wu wei, we do not impose any kind of extraneous force on a situation, because such force, by its very nature, is not in accord with the situation. For example, the people living in an urban slum are in a bad situation. They need better housing. But if we simply go in and knock the slum down and put in its place an architect's imaginative notion of a superefficient high-rise apartment building to "store" these people as if they were goods, we do not solve the problem; we create utter chaos. The slum, for all its shortcomings, has an ecosystem all of its own. It consists of a very complex system of relationships which make it a going concern, even though it may not be going very well, and anybody who wants to alter that situation must first become sensitive to all the conditions and interrelationships involved.

It is terribly important to become aware of the interdependence of every form of life upon every other form of life. This is how, for example, we cultivate the animals that we eat. We look after them, and feed them, and see that they breed in reasonable quantities. We do not do it very well, as a matter of fact, and troubles are arising about the supplies of fish in the ocean and many other species resulting from our poor or shortsighted husbandry. But in the greater ecosystem it is clear that the apparent conflict among various species is not actually a competition. Instead it is a very strange system of interrelationship, a system of things feeding on each other and cultivating each other at the same time. This is the idea of the friendly enemy, the necessary adversary who is part of life. You have conflicts going on in your own body, and all kinds of microorganisms are eating each other up, but if that were not happening you would not be healthy.

All the interrelationships of nature, whether they appear to be friendly relationships, as between bees and flowers, or conflicting relationships, as between birds and worms, are actually forms of cooperation. This is called "mutual arising." When you understand this as the basis of all existence and are able to act "without forcing," your life is spontaneous, a life which is so of itself, natural, not forced, and not unduly self-conscious.

Now another term that is important, although it has greater use in Neo-Confucian philosophy and Buddhism than in the writings of Lao-tzu, is *li*. This is a very useful concept in understanding the sort of natural order of mutual interdependence and mutual arising. Li originally meant the markings in jade, the grain in wood, or the fiber in muscle. It is defined nowadays in most dictionaries as "reason" or "principle," but this is not a very good translation. Joseph Needham once suggested that "organic pattern" was an ideal translation, and it is certainly preferable to "reason." The markings in jade are what make it beautiful, and as you look down at the ocean, you see patterns in the foam after a wave breaks. As you watch those patterns you know they will never make an aesthetic mistake. They are not symmetrical and are rather difficult to describe. They are wiggly, like the markings in jade and the grain in wood, which also reflect the fluid patterns of water.

All these things exhibit li, and they all have distinct forms that we can distinguish quite clearly from what we call a mess. The foam patterns of waves, the mineral patterns of jade, and the vegetable patterns of wood are extraordinarily orderly, yet they do not have an obvious order, and nobody can ever pin this organic order down completely. We know that it is order and that it is something quite different from a random mess, but there is no way of defining that order completely. To be able to paint that way, or live that way, or to deliver justice that way, you have to have that order within you innately. You have to have an essential sense of li, but there is no way of prescribing it. This is very difficult for teachers, because in all of our modern schools and universities we are attempting to teach creativity. The trouble is that if we found a method whereby we could teach creativity, and everybody could explain just how it was done, it would no longer be of interest. The mysterious, the dark black of lacquer, the impenetrable and profound depth out of which glorious things come, is always an essential element in the creative.

There is a poem that says, "When the bird calls, the mountain becomes more mysterious." Imagine that you are in a mountain valley and everything is silent; suddenly, somewhere off in the distance, an unseen crow caws. You do not know where the crow is, but its cry emphasizes the silence and heightens the sense of mystery. There is a Chinese poem written by a man who went to find a sage who lived in a little hut in the mountains, with a boy there to serve him: "I asked the boy beneath the pines. He said, 'The master has gone alone, herb gathering somewhere on the mount, cloud-hidden, whereabouts unknown.'"

The best teachers of athletic and artistic skills are those who teach without forcing. I once studied the piano, though I am absolutely no good at it now because I do not practice. But I had an absolutely superb teacher for a while, and he was a very great musicologist with the highest standards. When I first went to him he said, "Let me see what you can do." So I played a Scarlatti sonata, and he said, "The trouble is that you are trying too hard. You are hitting the piano, and one should never hit a piano." Actually, all you have to do in order to play a piano is to drop your hands on it, and to do this properly you need to have relaxed arms. He made me practice for a while and felt my muscles to see if I were relaxed or not, and then he said, "Now just drop your hands on the piano. I don't care which notes you hit, but just drop your hands, let them fall." There is enough energy in the weight in your arm to play as loud as you will or as soft as you will — just let them drop.

He kept feeling my arms. "No, no, you are getting too tense, you must pretend you are Lao-tzu," he said, for he was a very educated man and he knew about these things. After a while I was able to relax, and then he said, "Now, after dropping your hands all you have to do is hit the right notes." "You know, the same thing is involved in making a very complex trill," and he demonstrated. He just dropped his hand on the piano and at the same time his fingers went "flump," and produced a magnificent ornamentation. We went on and we practiced this for some time, and then he said, "Now let's get around to hitting the right notes."

Now let us return to the problem of thinking about thinking. Sometimes people are removed from life because they dwell entirely in the world of the intellect. They are living in a world of symbols. Intellectuals are in a way removed from life, tied up in their categories and catalogs, their musts and must-nots. Yet this realm is also real, and thinking about thinking can be lived with as much directness, freshness, and spontaneity as life without thinking. But in order to live in the realm of thinking about thinking with full spontaneity, we must no longer regard the symbol, the thought, the idea, or the word as a block to life, or a means of escape from life. To be able to use the symbol, but not as means of escape, you have to know that you cannot escape in the first place. Not only can you not escape, but there is no one to escape: there is no one to be delivered from the prison of life.

The liberation of the mind from symbols is exactly the same process as breaking up the links between successive moments and the illusion of a continuing self that travels from moment to moment. A continuing self is as much an illusion as a wave of moving water, or the appearance of a solid circle created by moving a light in the dark. The fallacy of the continuous self is pointed out by the saying, "No one perceives anything, and no one experiences anything — there is simply seeing and experiencing." In fact we introduce these redundancies through language when we talk about seeing sights, hearing sounds, and feeling feelings. There are sights, there are sounds, there are feelings. We do not feel a feeling; the feeling itself already contains the feeling of it. This is very simple. Sight does not depend on the existence of the seen and the seer, bound together by some mysterious process. The seer and the seen, the knower and the known, are what we call "terms." Terms mean ends, and these are in mathematical language called limits. Now, when we pick up a stick, the stick has two ends, and they are the limits of the stick. The ends of the stick do not exist as separate points, which encounter each other on the occasion of meeting at a stick. Actually, they are abstract points, and the ends in and of themselves are considered as purely geometrical Euclidian imaginations; the stick is the actual reality.

In the same way, in the phenomenon called experience reality is not an encounter of the knower and the known. Reality is the experience that can be termed as having two aspects, two ends, the knower and the known, although this is only a figure of speech. In a neurological sense, everything you see is yourself. What you are aware of is a state of your nervous system, and there is no other knowledge whatsoever. That does not mean that your nervous system is the only existing reality, and that there is nothing beyond your nervous system, but it does mean that all knowledge is knowledge of you, and that therefore, in some mysterious way, you are not different from the external world you know. If you see, then, that what you experience and what you are are the same thing, then take it a step further, and realize also that you are in the external world you are looking at. Just as I am in your external world, you are in my external world, and yet I am in the same world you are.

My inside is not separable from the outside world. It is something that the so-called outside world is doing, just as it is doing the tree, the ocean, and everything else in the outside world. Now, isn't that great! We have now completely eliminated the person in the trap, the one who either dominates the world or suffers under it. It has vanished, it never was there, and when that happens, you can play any life game you want. You can link the past, the present, and the future together and play roles, but have seen through the great social lie that one accumulates or owns experiences, whether memories, sights, sounds, or other people. We are always building ourselves as the haver of all this, but if you think that you have been had!

CHAPTER TEN

PHILOSOPHY OF NATURE

CONTRARY TO POPULAR BELIEF, Americans are not materialists, as I have said before. We are not people who love material, and by and large our culture is devoted to the transformation of material into junk as rapidly as possible. God's own junkyard! Therefore, it's a very important lesson for a wealthy nation — and all Americans are colossally wealthy by the standards of the rest of the world — to see what happens to material in the hands of people who love it.

You might say that in Japan, and in China to a certain extent, the underlying philosophy of life is a sort of spiritual materialism. In the East, there is not the divorce between soul and body, between spirit and matter, between God and nature, that there is in the West. Therefore, there is not the same kind of contempt for material things.

We regard matter as something that gets in our way, something with limitations that are to be abolished as quickly as possible. We have bulldozers and every kind of technical device for knocking material out of the way, and we like to do as much to obliterate time and space as possible. We talk about killing time and getting from one place to another as fast as possible.

This is one of the great difficulties facing Japan. What is going to happen to Japan when it becomes the same place as California? In other words, you can take a streetcar from one end of town to another, and it's the same town. So, if you can take a jet plane from one city to another, then they're going to become the same place. To preserve the whole world from ultimate Los Angelization, we in the United States have to learn how to enjoy material and to be true materialists, instead of exploiters of material. This is one of the main reasons for exploring the philosophy of the Far East and how it relates to everyday life — to architecture, to gardens, to painting, and to rituals like the tea ceremony.

Basic to all of this is the philosophy of nature. The Japanese philosophy of nature is probably founded on the Chinese philosophy of nature, so we'll begin there.

To let the cat out of the bag right at the beginning: The basic assumption underlying Far Eastern and East Indian cultures is that the whole cosmos, the whole universe, is one being. It is not a collection of many things that floated together like a lot of flotsam and jetsam from the ends of space and just happened to end up forming this thing we call the universe. Easterners look at the world as one eternal activity, and that's the only real self you have. You are the works, and that thing we call you, the so-called "separate organism," is simply a manifestation of the whole thing. And this is not just a theory, it is a feeling that they have.

The great masters of the Far East and India, whatever sphere they're in, are fundamentally of this feeling that what you are is the thing that always was, is, and will be. And this eternal thing is playing the games called "Mr. Tokano," or "Mr. Lee," or "Mr. Mukapadya." These are special games it's playing, just like there's the fish game, the grass game, the bamboo game, and the pine tree game. These are all ways of saying, "Hello. Look at me. Here I am. It's me!" And everything is doing a dance, only it's doing it according to its own nature and the nature of the dance. The universe is fundamentally all these dances, whether human, fish, bird, cloud, sky, or star. They are all one fundamental dance or dancer. In Chinese, however, one doesn't distinguish the noun from the verb in the same way that we do. A noun can become a verb; a verb can become a noun. Now, that's a civilized culture!

Above all, an enlightened person in Eastern culture is one who knows that his so-called "separate personality," his ego, is an illusion. Illusion doesn't mean a bad thing; it just means a play. From the Latin word *ludere*, we get the English word *illusion*, and *ludere* means to play. The Sanskrit word *maya*, meaning illusion, also means magic, skill, art. The Sanskrit concept comes through China to Japan with the transmission of Buddhism.

The East Indian vision of the world as a maya, or as it is sometimes called in Sanskrit, *lila*, is also a play. So, all individual manifestations are games, dances, symphonies, and musical forms of the whole show. And the underlying belief is that everyone is the whole show.

But nature, as the word is used in the East, does not mean quite the same thing as it does in the West. In Chinese, the word we translate as nature is *tse-jan*, and it is made up of two characters. The first one means "of itself," and the second one means "so." What is so, of itself.

This is a rather difficult idea to translate into English. We might say "automatic," but that suggests something mechanical. This is something that is of itself so — what happens, what comes naturally. It is our sense of the word *nature* insofar as it means to be natural, to act in accordance with one's nature, not to strive for things, not to force things. When your hair grows, it grows without your telling it to do so, and you don't have to force it to grow. In the same way, your eyes, whether they are blue or brown, color themselves, and you don't tell them how to do it. When your bones grow a certain way, they do it all of themselves.

I remember a Zen master who taught in New York. He was a beautiful man, and his name was Mr. Sasaki. One evening, he was sitting in his golden robes, in a very formal throne-like chair with a fan in his hand. He had one of those fly whisks made of a white horse's tail. He was looking very dignified, with incense burning on the table in front of him. There was a little desk and on it was one of the scriptures that he was explaining. He said, "All nature has no purpose. Purposelessness most fundamental principle of Buddhism; purposelessness. Ahh, when you drop a fart, you don't say, 'At nine o'clock I dropped a fart.' It just happens."

It is fundamental to this idea of nature that the world has no boss. This is very important, especially if you're going to understand Shinto. We translate *kami*, or *shin*, as God, but it's not God in that sense. God, in the common Western meaning of the word, means "the controller," "the boss of the world." And the model that we use for nature tends to be the model of the carpenter or potter or king. Just as the carpenter takes wood and makes a table out of it or as the potter takes inert clay and evokes a form in it or as the king tells people what order they shall move in and how they shall behave, it is ingrained in the Western mind to think that the universe is a behavior that is responding to somebody in charge — somebody who understands it all.

When I was a little boy, I used to ask my mother many questions. Sometimes she'd get fed up with me and say, "My dear, there are some things in this life that we are just not meant to know."

And so I said, "Well, what about it? Will we ever know?"

"Yes," she said. "When you die and you go to heaven, God will make it all clear."

And I used to think that maybe, on wet afternoons in heaven, we'd all sit around God's throne and say, "Oh, Heavenly Father, why are the leaves green?" And he would say, "Because of the chlorophyll!" And we would say, "Oh!"

Well, that idea — of the world as an artifact — could prompt a child in our culture to ask his mother, "How was I made?" And the question seems very natural. So when it's explained that God made you, the child naturally goes on and says, "But who made God?"

However, I don't think a Chinese child would ask the question, "How was I made?" And this is because the Chinese mind does not look at the world of nature as something manufactured, but rather grown. The character for coming into being in Chinese is based on the symbol of a growing plant, and growing and making are two different things. When you make something, you assemble parts or you take a piece of wood and you carve it, working gradually from the outside inward, cutting away until you've got the shape you want.

But when you watch something grow, it isn't like that. If you see, for example, a fast-motion movie of a rose growing, you will see that the process goes from the inside to the outside. It is, as it were, something expanding from the center. And far from being an addition of parts, it all moves together and grows out of itself all at once. The same is true when you watch the formation of crystals or a photographic plate being developed. Suddenly, all over the area of the plate, all over the field, the photo appears.

So the world as a self-generating organism does not obey laws in our sense of "the laws of nature," and in Chinese philosophy there is no difference between the *Tao* (in Japanese, *dō*), the way or power of nature, and the things in nature. Everything is said to have its own Tao, from which it acts according to its own nature. Of course, here I am using *nature* to mean the character or qualities of a thing and not something distinct from man.

When I stir up the air with a fan, it isn't simply that the air obeys the fan. There wouldn't even be a fan in my hand unless there were air around it. So unless there is air, there is no fan. The air brings the fan into being as much as the fan brings the air into being. Because the Taoists see the unity implied in the interdependence of things, they don't think of things as obeying all the time, of masters and slaves, of lords and servants.

Lao-tzu, who is supposed to have written the *Tao Te Ching*, the fundamental book of Taoist philosophy, is said to have lived in China around the time of Confucius. In his book, he wrote, "The great Tao flows everywhere, to the left and to the right. It loves and nourishes all things, but does not lord it over them. And when merits are attained, it makes no claim to them." Now it seems probable that this book was actually a collection of the wisdom of the day. And if this is the way nature is run, why not the government as well? By letting everything follow its course, the skillful man or woman — and also the skillful ruler — interferes as little as possible with the course of things.

Of course, for the reasons noted above, you can't help but interfere a little. Every time you look at something, you change it. Your very existence is, in a way, an interference, and if you think of yourself as something separate from the rest of the world, then you will think in terms of interference and noninterference. But if you know that you're not separate from it, that you are just as much in and of nature as the wind or the clouds, then who is it that interferes?

The same principle is seen in the notion that life is most skillfully lived when one sails a boat rather than rowing it. It's more intelligent to sail than to row. With oars I have to use my muscles and my effort to drag myself along the water. But with a sail, I let the wind do the work for me. And it is more skillful still when I learn to tack and let the wind blow me against the direction of the wind.

That balance of participation is the whole philosophy of the Tao. It's called, in Chinese, *wu wei*; *wu* is "non," and *wei* is "striving." *Mui* is the Japanese version of this concept. In Japanese, *mu* is the Chinese *wu*, and so in this context becomes mui, as distinct from *ui*. Ui means to use effort, that is, to go against the grain, to force things. So together they mean not to go against the grain, that is, to go with the grain. If you travel through Japan, you will see around you, in every direction, examples of mui, of the intelligent handling of nature so as to go with it rather than against it.

For example, the famous art of judo is entirely based on this principle. When you are attacked, you don't simply oppose the force used against you. Instead, you go in the same direction as the attack is headed, and lead it to its own downfall. This is the same strategy seen in the way a willow tree survives the winter. Nearby there is a strong pine tree that has a tough branch that reaches out, flexing its muscles. Then the snow piles up and up, and this unyielding branch holds a huge weight of snow. It cracks. However, the willow tree has a springy, supple branch, and when a little snow comes on it the branch just goes down. The snow falls off, and the branch goes up again.

Lao-tzu said, "Man, at his birth, is supple and tender. But in death, he is rigid and hard. Plants when they are young, are soft and supple. But in death, they are brittle and hard. So, suppleness and tenderness are the characteristics of life, and rigidity and hardness the characteristics of death." He made many references to water and said, "Of all things in the world, nothing is more soft than water, and yet it wears away the hardest rocks. Furthermore, water is humble; it always seeks the lowest level, which men abhor. But eventually, water overcomes everything in its path."

When you watch water take the line of least resistance and you see, for example, water poured out on the ground, you will see it projecting fingers from itself. Some of those fingers stop, but one finger goes on, because it has found the lowest level. Now, you might say, "Oh, but that's not the water. The water didn't do anything. That's just the contours of the land, and because of the contours of the land, the water goes where the land makes it go." But think again. Isn't it also the nature of water that makes it go?

I will never forget that once, when I was out in the countryside, a piece of thistledown flew out of the blue. It came right down to me, and I put out a finger, and I caught it by one of its little tendrils. Then it behaved just like a daddy longlegs; you know, when you catch one by the leg it naturally struggles to get away. Well, this little thing behaved just like that, and I thought, "It is just the wind doing that. It only appears as if the thistledown is doing that." But then I thought again, "It is the wind, yes, but it's also this thistledown that had the intelligence to grow itself so as to use the wind to help it get away." That little structure of thistledown exhibits a high form of intelligence, just as surely as the construction of a house that follows the contours of the land is a manifestation of a high level of human intelligence. But the thistledown is using the wind instead of the slope.

In much the same way, the water uses the conformations of the ground to get away. Water isn't just dead stuff. It's not just being pushed around. In fact, nothing is being pushed around in the Chinese view of nature. What they mean by nature is something that happens of itself; it has no boss. Nobody is giving orders, and so nobody is obeying orders. That leads further to an entirely different conception of cause and effect. Cause and effect is based on giving orders. When you say, "Something made this happen," you are saying it had to happen because of what happened before. But the Chinese don't think like that. Their concept, which does duty for our idea of causality, is called "mutual arising."

As an example, let's consider the relationship between the back and the front of anything. Is the back the cause of the front, or is the front the cause of the back? What a silly question! If things don't have fronts, then they can't have backs. If they don't have backs, they can't have fronts. Front and back always go together; that is to say, they come into being together. And so, in just the same way as the front and the back arise together, Taoist philosophy sees everything in the world arising together.

This is called the philosophy of mutual interpenetration — in Japanese, *jiji muge* — and it goes way back in history to the Chinese idea of nature. To look at it very simply, let us suppose that you had never seen a cat, and one day you were looking through a very narrow slit in a fence, and a cat walked by. First you would see the cat's head. Then there's a rather nondescript fuzzy interval, and then a tail follows. And you say, "Marvelous!" Then the cat turns around and walks back. You see the head, and then after a little interval, the tail. You might say, "My! That's just incredible! The head caused the tail." The cat then turns around and walks back, and again you see first the head and then the tail. So you say, "This has some regularity, and there must be some order in this phenomenon. Whenever I see the thing that I've labeled head, I then see the thing I've labeled tail. Therefore, where there is an event that I call 'head' and it's invariably followed by another event that I call 'tail,' obviously the head is the cause, and the tail is the effect."

We think that way about everything. But if you suddenly widened the crack in the fence, you would see that the head and the tail are all one cat. Like everything else that comes into being naturally, a cat is born with a head and a tail. In exactly the same way, the events that we seem to call "separate" are really all one event. But we chop it into pieces to describe it, just as we say, "The head of the cat and the tail of the cat," although it's all one head-tail cat. We've chopped it to pieces in order to describe it, but then we forget that we did that. We try to explain how the pieces fit together. So we have invented a myth called "causality" in order to explain how they do fit together.

We chop the world into bits as a matter of intellectual convenience. However, our world is very wiggly through and through, and you will notice how people, although they hold up models of symmetry as seen in most houses, love the wigglyness in their garden. Nature is fundamentally wiggly.

I remember as a child wondering why Chinese houses all had curved roofs, and why all the people in the landscapes looked more wiggly than ours. Finally I figured out that this is because they see that the world is wiggly! We say, "Now, what can you do with a wiggly world? You've got to straighten it out!" Always, our initial solution is to try and straighten things out.

Of course people are very wiggly indeed. It is only because we all appear pretty much the same that we look regular. We have two eyes, one nose, one mouth, two ears, and so on. We look regular, so we make sense. But if somebody had never seen a person before, he might ask, "What is this extraordinarily wiggly phenomenon? It seems to wiggle all over the place!"

One of the wiggliest things in the world is a fish. Somebody once found out they could use a net and catch a fish. Then they thought of an even better idea than that: They could catch the world with a net and use it to make sense of a wiggly world. But what happens if you hang up a net in front of the world and look through it? You can count the wiggles by saying, "This wiggle goes so many holes up, so many holes down, and so many holes across. It goes so many to the left and so many to the right." But what do you end up with? What you have as a result of this exercise is a calculus. Your net breaks up the world into countable bits.

In the same way, a bit is a bite of something, just as when you go to eat chicken, you can't swallow the whole chicken at once. To eat it you have to cut it into bites. But you don't get a cut-up fryer out of the egg. So in the same way the real universe has no bits. It's all one thing; it's not a lot of things. In order to digest it with your mind, which thinks of one thing at a time, you have to construct a calculus. So you chop the universe into bits, and you think about it, and talk about it one bit at a time.

You can see this whole page at once, but if you want to talk about it, you have to talk about it word by word, idea by idea, and bit by bit.

So to describe things, you go into all the details. But how does one select which details? Well now, if you don't realize that's what you've done, that you've "bitted" the world in order to think about it when it isn't really bitted at all, then you have troubles. Not only do you have to explain how the bits go together, but in order to explain how they connect with each other you have to invent all sorts of ghosts. Some of these ghosts are called "cause and effect," influences used to explain things. Indeed you may ask, "How do I influence you?" But what does this really mean? These influences — the ghosts and spooks we regard as things — only come into being if we forget that we made the initial step of breaking the unity into pieces in order to discuss it. That is, they are a part of the illusion.

Stepping back, we have these basic principles to consider. The world as nature, what happens of itself, is looked upon as a living organism. It doesn't have a boss because things are not behaving in response to something that pushes them around. They are just behaving, and it's all one big behavior. However, if you want to look at it from certain points of view, you can see it as if something else were making something happen, just as we looked at the cat through the slit in the fence. But you only see the parts because you divide the thing up.

This might lead you to ask, "In Chinese philosophy, is nature chaotic? Is there really no law?" There is no Chinese word that means the law of nature. The only word in Chinese that means law — *tse* — is a character that represents a cauldron with a knife beside it. It goes back to very ancient times, when a certain emperor made laws for the people. He had the laws etched on the sacrificial cauldrons so that when the people brought sacrifices they would read what was written on the cauldrons. But the sages, who were of a Taoist persuasion during the time that this emperor lived, said, "You shouldn't have done that, Sir, because the moment the people know what the law is, they become a little devious. And they'll say, 'Well now, did you really mean that precisely or did you mean this?' The next thing you know, they will find a way to wrangle around it." So they said that the nature of nature, Tao, is *wu-tse*, which means lawless.

But although we say that nature is lawless, this is not to say it is chaotic. The Chinese word for the order of nature is *li*. In Japanese, it is *ri*. Li is a curious word that originally meant "the markings in jade, the grain in wood, or the fiber in muscle." Now, when you look at jade and you see these wonderful, mottled markings, you know that somehow these markings are not chaotic, although you can't explain why. And when you look at the patterns of clouds or the bubbles of foam on the water, it's astounding, because they never make an aesthetic mistake.

Look at the stars. They are not arranged; instead they seem to be scattered through the heavens like sea spray. Yet you could never criticize stars for displaying poor taste, any more than you could criticize mountain ranges for having awkward proportions. These designs are spontaneous, and yet they demonstrate the wiggly patterns of nature that are quite different from anything you would call a mess. We can't quite put our finger on what the difference is between the two, but we certainly can see the difference between a tide pool and an ashtray full of garbage. We may not be able to define the difference, but we know they are different.

If you could define aesthetic beauty, however, it would probably cease to be interesting. That is, if we had a way of capturing it and a method that would automatically produce great artists — and anybody could go to school and become a great artist — art would soon become the most boring kind of expression. But precisely because you don't know how it's done, that gives spontaneous art a level of excitement.

And so it is with the philosophy of nature. There is no formula, no tse or rule according to which all this happens. And yet it's not a mess. So, this idea of li, or organic pattern, is the word that they use for the order of nature. Instead of our idea of law, where the things are obeying something, they are not obeying God in the sense of a governor. They are not following principles, like a streetcar that follows along the track.

Do you know that limerick about the streetcar?

There was a young man who said, "Damn!
For it certainly seems that I am
A creature that moves
In determinate grooves.
I'm not even a bus, I'm a tram!"

So that idea of the iron rails, along which the course of life goes, is absent in the East. And that accounts for a certain humanism that is very present in these cultures. The people in the Far East, and particularly in China and Japan, never feel guilty. They may feel ashamed because they have transgressed social requirements, but they do not have the sense of guilt that we generally equate with sinfulness. They don't feel, as with the idea of original sin, that you are guilty because you owe your existence to the Lord God — or perhaps you were a mistake anyway! They don't feel that. They have social shame, but not metaphysical guilt, and that leads to a great relaxation. You can feel it, if you're sensitive, just walking around the streets. You realize that these people have not been tarred with that terrible monotheistic brush that gives one the sense of guilt.

Instead they work on the supposition that human nature, like all nature, although it consists of the passions as much as the virtues, is essentially good. In Chinese the word *un* means human-heartedness, or humanness, but not in the sense of being humane out of a kind of necessity, but of being human. So when I say, "Oh, he's a great human being," I mean he's the kind of person who's not a stuffed shirt, who is able to come off it, who can talk with me as a person, and who recognizes that he is a rascal, too. And so when a man, for example, affectionately calls a friend "you old bastard," this is a term of endearment, because he knows that "the old bastard" shares with him what I call the "element of irreducible rascality" that we all have.

So then, if a person has this attitude, he is never going to be an overbearing goody-goody. Confucius said, "Goody-goodies are the thieves of virtue." Because the philosophy of the goody-goody is, "If I am right, then you are wrong, and we will get into a fight. What I am is a crusader against the wrong, and I'm going to obliterate you, or I'm going to demand your unconditional surrender." But if I say, "No, I'm not right, and you're not wrong, but I happen to want to win. You know, you've got the most beautiful temples and I'm going to fight you for them." But if I had done that, I would be very careful not to destroy the temples. However in modern warfare we don't care. The only people who are safe are in the air force, because they are way up there. The women and children will be gone, because they can be frizzled with a Hiroshima bomb. But we in the plane will be safe. Now this is inhuman because we are fighting for idealogy instead of for practical things like food, and for possessions, and for greed.

So this is why the Chinese recognize both sides of human nature, and a Confucian would say he trusts human passions more than he trusts human virtues: righteousness, goodness, principles, and all that highfalutin abstraction. Let's get down to earth; let's come off it. And this, then, is why there is a kind of man in whom trust is put, because he recognizes the kind of nature that human nature is. If you are like the Christians who don't trust human nature — who say, "It's fallen, it's evil, it's perverse" — that puts you in a very funny position. If you say, "Human nature is not to be trusted," then you can't even trust the fact that you don't trust it! And do you see where you'll end up?

Now, it's true that human nature is not always trustworthy, but you must proceed on the gamble that it's trustworthy most of the time, or at least 51 percent of the time. Because if you don't, what's your alternative? You have to have a police state, and everybody has to be watched and controlled. But then who's going to watch the police? So, you end up the way they did in China just before 250 B.C. when there was the Chi'in Dynasty that lasted fifteen years. The emperor decided that everything would be completely controlled in order to make his dynasty last for a thousand years. In the process, he made a mess. So the Han Dynasty, which lasted from 206 B.C. to A.D. 220, came into being, and the first thing they did was abolish all laws, except those about elementary violence and robbery. But all of the complexity of law was removed, and historically the Han Dynasty marked the height of Chinese civilization. It was a period of real peace and great sophistication. It was China's Golden Age, although I may be oversimplifying it a bit, as all historians do.

This marvelous reign was based on the whole idea of the humanism of the Far East, recognizing that although human beings are scalawags, they are no more so than cats and dogs and birds. So you must trust human nature, because if you can't, you're apt to starve.

CHAPTER ELEVEN

SWIMMING HEADLESS

THE SECOND WORD IN THE TITLE of Lao-tzu's *Tao Te Ching* presents us with some serious problems in translation. *Te* is ordinarily translated "virtue," but virtue as we understand it today isn't at all appropriate. Te means virtue in the sense that we speak of the healing virtues of a plant. In the section of the Lao-tzu where the term is introduced the text reads, literally, "Superior virtue, not virtue, thus it has virtue. The idea of virtue cannot let go of virtue, thus it is not virtue." A smoother translation is, "Superior virtue is not conscious of itself as virtue, therefore it is virtue. The idea of virtue is so hooked on being virtuous that it is not virtue." Te means the excellence of things in the sense that a tree excels at being a tree. There is no way to imitate a tree; the only way is to be one. In the same way, when a human being shows extraordinary skill at something it seems that it comes naturally to him. Nothing artificial is apparent, and if there is some discipline involved, it is concealed. Such artless excellence seems like magic, and in te there is a connection between virtue and magic.

Everything is fundamentally in harmony with the Tao. It is said the Tao is that from which nothing can depart, and that from which things can depart is not the Tao. Fundamentally, then, we cannot get away from it. It is as if we are all floating in a tremendous river, which carries us along. Some people may swim against the river, yet they are still being carried along. Others have learned the art of swimming with the river. They are carried along too, but they are aware of it. They know they are being carried along, whereas the people who are swimming against the river *think* they are going in the opposite direction, though they're not, really. We have to flow with the river; there is no other way. We can swim against it, and pretend not to be flowing with it, but we still are. What's more, the person who gives up that pretense, who realizes one is inevitably carried by the river and swims with it, suddenly acquires behind everything they do the force of the river. The person swimming against the river does not by his action express the power of the river. On the other hand the person swimming with it rides the river's force and has behind them the whole river, the power of which they can subtly direct. They can change direction in the river, going to the left or the right as a ship uses a rudder to steer in the current; or if he is more skillful still, he can tack. When a sailboat tacks, it sails against the wind, yet it still uses the wind to blow it along. That is the most skilled art of all; that is perfection in Taoism.

Te is a kind of intelligence that invites cooperation, so that the desired end is accomplished without unnecessary effort. For example, instead of forcing others to agree with you, you can give them the notion that the idea you want them to have is their own. In the same way when you want to teach a baby to swim, you can put the baby in the water and then move backwards with the baby to create a vacuum. This pulls the baby along, and it learns the feel of the water and, eventually, how to swim on its own.

The *Tao Te Ching* is a book written for several purposes. We may take it as a guide to mystical understanding of the universe, or we may take it as a dissertation on the principles of nature, almost a handbook of natural law. We may also take it as a political treatise, a book of wisdom for governors, and on this subject the basic principle that it advocates is the virtue of governing by not ruling. Suppose the president of the United States were as unknown to you by name as the local sanitary inspector, the person who looks after the drains and the sewage disposal. The inspector may not be a glamorous figure, but for that very reason he probably does his job more efficiently than the president. The president wastes an enormous amount of time meeting with various groups, conferring honors, and so forth, and with all of the ceremonial functions the poor man's life must be an utter torment. He is so well known that he has little time to give to the government of the country. Just think of his mail, and all the people who have to be employed sifting it out and assessing it. If he were someone quite anonymous, so that we did not have to think about him, he would be a very good ruler in just the same way, for example, as are the systems that govern your own body's functions. You do not have to attend to your body unless you are sick. The government of your body happens automatically, going on day after day after day. The better it is the less you have to think about it. On the deepest level, a person can get in the way of his own existence by becoming too aware of himself. Such a person lacks the quality of te.

The Taoists propose to help people get back to Tao, and the state of te, so that they will not get in their own way. The key, they say, is in the idea of being empty. Emptiness, being vacant, is the secret of all things. The highest kind of knowledge is not "know-how" but "no how" — to be able to achieve things with "no how" — that is, without any method. This is done through something called "fasting the heart." The Chinese word *hsin* is translated as "heart" but does not mean heart in the physiological sense. Pronounced "shin," it is in fact a part of the character te, and its meaning is closer to "heart-mind" or "psychic center." Hsin is also frequently translated as "mind," and in all the Zen texts where the term "no mind" is used the actual word is *wu hsin* (Japanese, *mushin*). The most desirable kind of heart, then, is absence of heart. In English, "heartless" has very bad connotations, as does "mindless." A heartless person is an inconsiderate and unfeeling person, and a mindless person is an idiot, but in Chinese Buddhism and Taoism, a person who has mushin, no mind or no heart, is a person of a very high order. His psychic center does not get in its own way, and it operates as if it was not there.

Lao-tzu said that "the highest form of man uses his hsin like a mirror — it grasps nothing, it refuses nothing, it receives but does not keep." And the poem says, "When the geese fly over the water and they are reflected in the water, the geese do not intend to cast their reflection and the water has no mind to retain their image." The art of living is to operate in the world as if you were absent. As a matter of fact, this is built into us physiologically. Let me ask you simply: What is the color of your head from the standpoint of your eyes? You feel that your head is black, or that it has not any color at all. Outside you see your field of vision as an oval because your two eyes act as two centers of an ellipse. But what is beyond the field of vision? What color is it where you can't see? It is not black, and this is an important point; there is no color at all beyond your field of vision. This little mental exercise gives us an idea of what is meant by the character *hsüan*. Although its dictionary definition is "dark, deep, obscure," it actually refers to this kind of no color that is the color of your head — as far as your eyes are concerned. Perhaps we could say that the invisibility of one's head, in a certain sense the lack of a head, is the secret of being alive. To be headless, or to have no head in just the sense I am talking about, is our way of talking about the Chinese expression wu hsin, or "no mind." As a matter of fact, if you want to see the inside of your head all you have to do is keep your eyes open, because all that you are experiencing in the external, visual field is a state of your brain.

All the colors and shapes you see are the way in which the brain nerves translate the electrical impulses in the external world outside the envelope of the skin. They translate all of what is going on outside into impulses, which are to us shape and color. However, shape and color are states of the nerves, so that what you see when your eyes are open is how it feels inside your head. You do not see your brain as an internal undulating structure; you see your brain as everything outside. In this way the emptiness of one's head is a condition of seeing, and the transparency of the eye lens is the condition of seeing colors. The thirteenth-century mystic Meister Eckhart said: "Because my eye has no color it is able to discern color"; and this is a restatement of the fundamental Taoist idea of being absent as a condition of being present, being not there so as to be there. Lao-tzu says, "When your belt is comfortable you don't feel it, when your shoes are comfortable it is as if you were not wearing any." The more aware you are of these things the less well they are made or the less well they fit.

We may raise a very simple objection to this, which is that if I do not know I am there I seem to be missing everything. We want to know that we know. If we are happy and we do not know we are happy we might just as well not be happy. To know that you are happy is really the overflowing of the cup of life. The downside of this principle is to be miserable and know that you are miserable. Some people are miserable without knowing it, but you know my limerick:

There was a young man who said, though
It seems that I know that I know
What I would like to see
Is the I that knows me
When I know that I know that I know

Of course this is the great human predicament, the development of self-consciousness, the development of the possibility of
reflecting upon one's own knowledge, which is simultaneously a
blessing and a curse. Taoism does not escape this problem and it
does not avoid it. It deals with it, but it does not deal with it obviously; it floats lightly over it.

Lao-tzu said, "It is easy enough to stand still; the difficulty is to
walk without touching the ground." He is referring to the fact that
in the state of being in accord with the Tao there is a certain feeling
of weightlessness, parallel to the weightlessness that people feel
when they float in space or when they go deep down into the ocean.
This is of course connected with the sensation that you are not carrying your body around, which I compare to the experience of an
expert driver when he really is "with it" in a car. When the hill lifts
him up and drops him off the other side there is a sense of weightlessness, and he and the road are all one process. Then of course
there is the song, "Walking on air, never a care, something is making me sing, tra-la-la-la, tra-la-la-la, like a little bird in spring."

What is this weightlessness? It means that you are not moving
around in constant opposition to yourself. Most people move in
constant opposition to themselves because they are afraid that if
they do not oppose themselves all the time they will lose control
and something awful will happen. When the human being developed the power to be aware of himself, to know that he knows —
in other words when the cortex was formed over the original brain

— he fell from grace. That was the fall of man, because when he felt the sensation of being in charge, of being in control of himself, he became anxious. Am I aware enough of myself? Have I taken enough factors into consideration? Have I done all that should be done? When he asked these questions of himself for the first time, he started to tremble, and this was the fall of man. This is also what Lao-tzu means when he says, "When the great Tao was lost there came duty to man and right conduct." In other words, nobody talks about how you ought to behave unless things have gone radically wrong. There would not be any conception of faithful ministers of the state unless there were a lot of lousy politicians around. No one would talk about filial piety unless there were wayward sons and daughters. According to the Taoists, moral preaching is the source of confusion. There is a marvelous story about a conversation between Confucius and Lao-tzu in which Lao-tzu asked Confucius to explain to him about charity and duty to one's neighbor. In reply Confucius gave him a little sermon on giving up self-interest and working for others, to which Lao-tzu replied, "What stuff sir! Regard the universe. The stars come out invariably every night, the sun rises and sets, the birds flock and migrate without exception, all flowers and trees grow upwards without exception. You with your 'charity' and 'duty to one's neighbor,' you are just introducing confusion into the realm. Your attempt to eliminate self is a manifestation of selfishness. You are like a person beating a drum in search of a fugitive." All talk about selfishness and all talk about becoming virtuous or enlightened or integrated or non-neurotic or self-actualized attests to the fact that it has not happened, and such talk will in fact get in the way of its happening.

The Taoist sage Lieh-tzu, who lived somewhat later than Lao-tzu, was known for his ability to ride on the wind. Before acquiring this skill, Lieh-tzu found a very great master and went to study with him. The master lived in a small hut and Lieh-tzu sat outside the hut, but the master paid absolutely no attention to him. Of course this is the way with Taoist masters. Why would they want students, since they have nothing to teach? After a year of sitting outside, Lieh-tzu went away because he was fed up with waiting so long. Then he became regretful about leaving and thought he really should make an attempt, so he went back to the master. When the master saw him approach, he asked, "Why this ceaseless coming and going?" So Lieh-tzu sat there and tried to control his mind so that he would not think of the difference between gain and loss, so that he could live in such a way that nothing is either an advantage or a disadvantage.

There is a marvelous story about this perspective. Once upon a time there was a Chinese farmer whose horse ran away, and all the neighbors came around to commiserate that evening. "So sorry to hear your horse has run away. This is most unfortunate." The farmer said, "Maybe." The next day the horse came back bringing seven wild horses with it, and everybody came back in the evening and said, "Oh, isn't that lucky. What a great turn of events. You now have eight horses!" And the farmer said, "Maybe." The next day his son tried to break one of these horses and ride it but he was thrown, and broke his leg, and they all said, "Oh dear, that's too bad," and he said, "Maybe." The following day the conscription officers came around to conscript people into the army and they rejected his son because he had a broken leg. Again all the people came around and said, "Isn't that great!" And he said, "Maybe."

The farmer steadfastly refrained from thinking of things in terms of gain or loss, advantage or disadvantage, because one never knows. Receiving a letter from a law office tomorrow saying that some distant relative of yours has left you a million dollars might make you feel very happy, but the windfall may well lead to unbelievable disaster — including a visit from the Internal Revenue

Service, just to mention one possibility. In fact we never really know whether an event is fortune or misfortune, we only know our ever-changing reactions to ever-changing events. The Taoist is wise enough to understand eventually that there is not any fixed good or bad; this point of view is called nonchoosing.

To return to Lieh-tzu, he attempted to keep his mind in a state of nonchoosing, but it is very difficult to overcome one's habits of feeling and thinking. After he had practiced this for a year, the master looked at him and recognized he was there. After another year's practice, the master invited him to come and sit inside his hut. Then something changed, and Lieh-tzu did not try to control his mind anymore. He described what he did: "I let my ears hear whatever they wanted to hear, I let my eyes see whatever they wanted to see, I let my feet move anywhere they wanted to go, I let my mind think of whatever it wanted to think, and it was a very strange sensation because all my bodily existence seemed to melt, and become transparent, and to have no weight. I didn't know whether I was walking on the wind or the wind was walking on me."

We insist, however, that there are events; we observe events, we remember events, and they make an impression on us. Yet in the psychology of Taoism there is no difference between the observer and what is observed. We are only the observation of life from a certain point of view. We create an opposition between the thinker and the thought, the experiencer and the experience, and the knower and the known because we think about knowledge in terms of certain metaphors — the metaphor of the stylus on the writing sheet, the reflection on the mirror. All those sorts of images are part of our idea of knowledge, but the Taoist theory of knowledge is quite different. There is no knower facing the known, and if there is any knower at all it contains the known. Your mind, if you have one, is not in your head; instead, your head is in your mind, because your mind, understood from the standpoint of vision, is space. The Chinese use the word *kung*, which means sky, space, or emptiness. *Se* means both shape and color. The famous lines of the *Heart Sutra* declare that "Space/emptiness *is precisely* shape/color and shape/color is *precisely* space/emptiness." What we call space contains the myriads of shapes and colors and bodies and weights and so on. It does not reflect them as a mirror; but it is the absence which guarantees their presence and it is their presence which guarantees absence. There is a mutual arising between voidness and form, between existence and nonexistence, being and nonbeing, and these are never felt as alternatives or elements that are in some kind of contest. When we say, then, that there is not any thinker behind thoughts, nor any experiencer that has experiences, this is a way of saying that experiencing or knowing is not an encounter between strangers.

Western thought concentrates very much on knowledge as an encounter, and talks about facing facts, facing reality, as if somehow or other the knower and the known came from two completely different worlds and met each other. The phenomenon of knowledge is almost the precise opposite of that. Instead of being a collision between two wandering bodies in space, knowledge is much more like the expansion of a flower from its stem, where stem and flower are knower and the known, the expression of something that lies between them. We tend in all our metaphors and common speech to think of life as a process that has polarized itself, coming out from a center and expressing itself in terms of opposites.

Of course this is the basis of the whole yang/yin principle illustrated as two interlocked fishes. It is a fascinating emblem because it is a helix, and it is the formation of a spiral nebula, and it is the position of sexual intercourse. I am trying to get to the middle of you, you are trying to get to the middle of me, neither one of us exist without the other. The yang is the light and yin is the dark. Yang originally meant the sunny south side of a mountain, and yin the dark north side. Yang is the north bank of a river, which gets the sun, yin is the south bank, which is in the shade. Now, there are no mountains with only one side. The mountain, if it is a mountain at all, goes up and down, like a wave. There are no waves with a crest but no trough or a trough with no crest, because you cannot have half a wave. Yang and yin are quite different from each other but just because they are different they are identical, and this is the important idea of the "identical difference."

The saying in both Taoism and Buddhism is that "difference is identity, identity is difference." The Chinese word for "is" is not quite the same as our word. It somewhat resembles "that," so we might render the statement "difference that identity, identity that difference." This does not mean quite A *is* B, but that A *is in relation to* B or A *goes with* B, or A *necessarily involves* B. Difference necessarily involves identity, identity necessarily involves difference, so there is no yang without yin, and there is no yin without yang. When I was first studying these things I was terribly bothered by how on earth I was going to see this multidifferentiated world as a unity. What was going to happen, what was it going to be like to see that all things are one? The sages keep saying all things are one, but they all look so different to me. All these people act in different ways, and they have all their houses and their cars and all their this and that. The whole world looked full of the most bony, prickly differences. I thought, "Well, what is supposed to happen? Is this supposed to be as if your eyesight blurred and all these things floated together? What is this experience of nirvana or of liberation supposed to be? Why do the Hindu sages write about it just as if it was a kind of dissolution of everything?" It took me a long time, and suddenly one day I realized that the difference I saw between things was the same thing as their unity, because differences, borders, lines, surfaces, boundaries do not really divide things from each other at all, they join them together, and all boundaries are held in common. It is like a territory that has all been divided up into property, and this is your property, and this is my property. But if I live next to you, your fence is my fence, and we hold the boundary in common. We may make up silly arrangements as to who is responsible for the maintenance of this fence, but nevertheless we hold our boundaries in common, and we would not know where my plot of land was unless we knew the definition of your plot of land, and the plot of land that is adjoining. I saw then that my sense of me being me was exactly the same thing as my sensation of being one with the whole cosmos. I did not need to have some other sort of different, odd kind of experience to feel in total connection with everything. Once you get the clue you see that the sense of unity is inseparable from the sense of difference. You would not know yourself, or what you meant by self, unless at the same time you had the feeling of other.

Now the secret is that the other eventually turns out to be you. The element of surprise in life is when suddenly you find the thing most alien turns out to be yourself. Go out at night and look at the stars and realize that they are millions and billions of miles away, vast conflagrations far out in space. You can lie back and look at that and say, "Well, surely I hardly matter. I am just a tiny little speck aboard this weird spotted bit of dust called earth, and all that was going on out there billions of years before I was born and will still be going on billions of years after I die." Nothing seems stranger to you than that, or more different from you, yet there comes a point, if you watch long enough, when you will say, "Why that's me!" It is the other that is the condition of your being yourself, as the back is the condition of being the front, and when you know that, you know you never die.

CHAPTER TWELVE

ZEN BONES

ONCE UPON A TIME, there was a Zen student who quoted an old Buddhist poem to his teacher:

> The voices of torrents are from one great tongue.
> The lines of the hills are the pure body of Buddha.

"Isn't that right?" he asked. "It is," said the teacher, "but it's a pity to say so."

It would be much better if this occasion were celebrated with no talk at all. If I addressed you in the manner of the ancient teachers of Zen, I should hit the microphone with my fan and leave. But I have the feeling that since you have contributed to the support of the Mountain Zen Center in expectation of learning something, a few words should be said, even though I warn you that by explaining these things to you I shall subject you to a very serious hoax. Now, if I allow you to leave here this evening under the impression that you understand something about Zen, you will have missed the point entirely. Zen is a way of life; a state of being that is not possible to embrace in any concept whatsoever.

Any concepts, any ideas, any words that I shall put across to you this evening will have as their object showing the limitations of words and of thinking. If one must try to say something about what Zen is, and I want to do this by way of introduction, I must emphasize that Zen in its essence is not a doctrine. There is nothing you are supposed to believe in, and it is not a philosophy in our sense; that is to say, it is not a set of ideas, an intellectual net in which one tries to catch the fish of reality. Actually, the fish of reality is more like water: it always slips through the net, and in water, when you get into it, there is nothing to hang onto. Of course this entire universe is like water; it is fluid, it is transient, it is changing. When you are thrown into the water after being accustomed to living on the dry land and you are not used to the idea of swimming, you try to stand on the water. You try to catch hold of it, and as a result you drown. This refers particularly to the waters of modern philosophical confusion, where God is dead, metaphysical propositions are meaningless, and there is really nothing to hang onto because we are all just falling apart. The only way to survive under those circumstances is to learn how to swim; you relax, you let go, and you give yourself to the water. You have to know how to breathe in the right way, but then you find that the water holds you up, and indeed in a certain way, you become the water.

If one attempts (again, I say, misleadingly) to put Zen into any sort of concept, it simply comes down to this: that in this universe there is one great energy, and we have no name for it. People have tried various names for it, such as God, Brahman, and Tao, but in the West the word God has so many funny associations attached to it that most of us are bored with it. When people say, "God the Father Almighty," most people feet funny inside, and so we like to hear new words. We like to hear about Tao, about Brahman, and about *tathata*, and other strange names from the Far East because they do not carry the same associations of mawkish sanctimony and funny meanings from the past. Actually, some of the words that the Buddhists use for the basic energy of the world really do not mean anything at all. The word *tathata*, which is Sanskrit for "suchness" or "vastness," really means something more like "da-da-da," based on the word *tat*, which in Sanskrit means "that." In Sanskrit existence is described as *tat tvam asi*, "Thou art that," or in modern American, "You're it." But da-da is the first sound a baby makes when it comes into the world because the baby looks around and says, "da, da, da, da, da." "That, that, that, that, that!" Fathers flatter themselves and think their baby is saying "da-da" for "daddy," but according to Buddhist philosophy this entire universe is one da-da-da, which means ten thousand functions, ten thousand things, or one suchness, and we are all one suchness.

Suchness comes and goes like everything else because this whole world is an on and off system. The Chinese say it is the yang and the yin and therefore it consists of now you see it, now you don't; here you are, here you aren't. It is the very nature of energy to be like waves, and of course waves have crests and troughs. However, we, being under a certain kind of sleepiness or illusion, imagine that the trough is going to overcome the wave or the crest; the yin, the dark principle, is going to overcome the yang, or the light principle, and that off is finally going to triumph over on. We "bug ourselves" by indulging in that illusion. "Supposing that darkness did win out, wouldn't that be terrible?" We are constantly worrying and thinking that it may, because after all, is it not odd that anything exists? It is most peculiar, it requires effort, it requires energy, and it would be so much easier for there to have been nothing at all. Therefore we think that since being, since the *is* side of things is so much effort, we will give up after a while and sink back into death. But death is just the other face of energy. It is the rest, the absence of anything around that produces something around, just as you cannot have solid without space, or space without solid. When you wake up to this, you realize that, as the French say, the more it changes, the more it is the same thing. You are really a playing of this one energy and there is nothing else but that. It is you, but for you to always be you would be an insufferable bore, and therefore it is arranged that you stop being you after a while and then come back as someone else altogether. When you find that out, you become full of energy and delight, and as Blake said, "Energy is eternal delight." Suddenly, you see through the whole sham of things and you realize you are that and you cannot be anything else, so you are relieved of fundamental terror. Of course, this does not mean that you are always going to be a great hero, or that you will not jump when you hear a bang, that you will not worry occasionally, or that you will not lose your temper. It means, though, that fundamentally, deep, deep down within you, you will be able to be human and not a stone Buddha. In Zen, there is a distinction made between a living Buddha and a stone Buddha. If you approach a stone Buddha and you hit him hard on the head, nothing happens except you break your fist or your stick. If you hit a living Buddha, he will say, "Ouch," and he will feel pain, because if he did not feel something, he would not be a human being.

Buddhas are human. They are not *devas*; they are not gods. They are enlightened men and women, but the point is that they are not afraid to be human. They are not afraid to let themselves participate in the pains, difficulties, and struggles that naturally go with human existence. It may seem almost an undetectable difference, and it takes one to know one. As the Zen poem says, "When two Zen masters meet each other on the street they need no introduction.

When thieves meet they recognize one another instantly." So, a person who understands Zen does not go around saying, "Oh, I understand Zen," "I have satori," or, "I have this attainment or that attainment," because if they did they would not understand the first thing about it. Chuang-tzu said, "The perfect man employs his mind as a mirror; it grasps nothing, it refuses nothing, it receives but does not keep." Yet another poem says of wild geese flying over a lake, "The wild geese do not intend to cast their reflection, and the water has no mind to retain their image." In other words, to put it in the contemporary idiom, this is to live without hang-ups. The word "hang-up" is almost an exact translation of the Sanskrit *klesha*, ordinarily translated as "worldly attachment." All that sounds a little bit pious, and in Zen things that sound pious are said to stink of Zen. However to have no hang-up is to be able to drift like a cloud and flow like water, seeing that all life is a magnificent illusion, a playing of energy, and there is absolutely nothing fundamentally to be afraid of. You will be afraid on the surface, you will be afraid of putting your hand in the fire, and you will be afraid of getting sick, but you will not be afraid of fear. Fear will pass over your mind like a black cloud, which flows through space without leaving any track.

That fundamental clarity is called the "void" in Buddhism, which does not mean void in the ordinary sense of emptiness. It means the void, which is the most real thing there is, though nobody can conceive it. The relation between the void and the world is like that you have between the speaker in a radio and all the various sounds that it produces.

On the speaker you hear human voices, you hear every kind of musical instrument, honking of horns, the sound of traffic, the explosion of guns, and this tremendous variety of sounds is the vibrations of one diaphragm, but it never says so. The announcer does not come on first thing in the morning and say, "Ladies and gentlemen, all the sounds that you will hear subsequently during the day will be the vibrations of this diaphragm, so do not mistake them for reality." The radio never mentions its own construction, and in exactly the same way you are never able really to make your mind an object of your own examination, just as you cannot look directly into your own eyes and you cannot bite your own teeth. You are your mind, and if you try to find it and make it something to possess it shows that you do not really know you are it. If you are it you do not need to make anything of it because there is nothing to look for, but the test is, are you still looking? Do you know that?

This knowing is not a kind of knowledge that you possess, not something you have learned in school, not something a degree testifies to. In this knowledge there is nothing to be remembered and nothing to be formulated. You know it best when you say, "Well, I don't know it," because that means you are not holding onto it and trying to cling to it in the form of a concept. There is absolutely no necessity to do so, and should you try, you would be, in Zen language, "putting legs on a snake" or a "beard on a eunuch," or as we would say, "gilding the lily." This sounds pretty easy, doesn't it? You mean to say all we have to do is just relax? We do not have to go around chasing anything anymore, we abandon religion, we abandon meditation, we abandon this, that, and the other, and just go on and live it up any way we like. This is what a father says to a child who keeps asking, "Why, why, why?" "Why did God make the universe?" "Who made God?" "Why are the trees green?" The father says finally, "Oh shut up and eat your bun." But it is not quite like that. All those people who try to realize Zen by doing nothing about it are still trying desperately to find it and are on the wrong track. There is another poem that says, "You cannot attain it by thinking, you cannot grasp it by not thinking," or you could say, "You cannot catch hold of the meaning of Zen by doing something about it, but equally you cannot see into its meaning by doing nothing about it." Both are in their different ways attempts to move from where you are now, here, to somewhere else.

The point is that we come to an understanding of what I call "suchness" only through being completely here, and no means are necessary to be completely here, either active means on the one hand or passive means on the other, because in both ways you are trying to move away from the immediate now.

It is difficult to understand language like that, however, and to understand what it is about, there is really one absolutely necessary prerequisite, and that is to stop thinking. Now, I am not saying this in the spirit of being an anti-intellectual, because I think a lot, talk a lot, write a lot of books, and am a sort of half-baked scholar. Yet, you know that if you talk all the time, you will never hear what anybody else has to say, and therefore all you will have to talk about is your own conversation. The same is true for people who think all the time, and I use the word *think* to mean talking to yourself, subvocal conversation, the constant chitchat of symbols and images and talk and words inside your skull. Now, if you do that all the time, you will find that you have nothing to think about except thinking, and just as you have to stop talking to hear what others have to say, you have to stop thinking to find out what life is about. The moment you stop thinking, you come into immediate contact with what Alfred Korzybski called so delightfully "the unspeakable world" — that is to say, the nonverbal world. Some people would call it the physical world, but these words *physical*, *nonverbal*, and *material* are all conceptual, and it is not a concept. It is not a noise either; it is simply this.

So, when you are awake to that world, you suddenly find that all the so-called differences between self and other, life and death, pleasure and pain, are all conceptual and they are not there. They do not exist at all in that world which is simply this. In other words, if I hit you hard enough, "Ouch!" does not hurt. If you are in the state of what is called "no thought," there is a certain experience, but you do not call it "hurt." It is like when you were small, and children banged you about and you cried and they said, "Don't cry," because they wanted to make you hurt and not cry at the same time. That is the reason why there is in Zen the practice of *zazen*, or sitting Zen.

In Buddhism they speak of the four dignities of man, walking, standing, sitting, and lying; and incidentally, there are three other kinds of Zen besides zazen: standing Zen, walking Zen, and lying Zen. They say, "When you sit just sit, when you walk just walk, but whatever you do, do not wobble." In fact, of course, you can wobble if you really wobble well.

When the old master Hyakujo was asked what Zen is, he said, "When hungry, eat. When tired, sleep." His questioner countered, "Well, isn't that what everybody does? Aren't you just like ordinary people?" "Oh no," he said, "they don't do anything of the kind. When they are hungry they don't just eat, they think of all sorts of things. When they're tired they don't just sleep, but dream all sorts of dreams." I know the Jungians will not like that, but there comes a time when you just dream yourself out, and there are no more dreams, and you sleep deeply and breathe from your heels. That is what makes zazen, or sitting Zen, a very good thing in the Western world. We have been running around far too much. It is all right because we have been active and our action has achieved a lot of good things. Yet, as Aristotle pointed out long ago, and this is one of the good things about Aristotle, "The goal of action is contemplation." In other words, busy, busy, busy, but what is it all about? When people are busy, they think they are going somewhere and that they are going to get somewhere and attain something. There is quite a point to action if you know you are not going anywhere, and if you act like you dance, or like you sing, or play music, then you are really not going anywhere. You are just doing pure action, but if you act with the thought that as a result of action you are eventually going to arrive at some place where everything will be all right, then you are on the exercise wheel of a squirrel cage, hopelessly condemned to what the Buddhists call *samsara*, the round or rat race of birth and death, because you think you are going to get somewhere. You are already there, and it is only a person who has discovered that they are already there who is capable of action. That person does not act frantically with the thought that he or she is going to get somewhere, and can go into walking meditation at that point, where we walk not because we are in a great hurry to get to a destination, but because the walking itself is great and the walking itself is the meditation.

When you watch Zen monks walk it is very fascinating, because they have a different kind of walk from everybody else in Japan. Most people shuffle along, or if they wear Western clothes, they race and hurry like we do. Zen monks have a peculiar swing when they walk, and you have the feeling they walk rather the same way as a cat. There is something about it that is not hesitant, they are going along all right, but they are walking just to walk, and one cannot act creatively except on the basis of stillness, of having a mind that is from time to time capable of stopping thinking.

The practice of sitting may seem very difficult at first, because if you sit in the Buddhist way, it makes your legs ache and most Westerners start to fidget because they find it very boring to sit for a long time. However, the reason they find it boring is that they are still thinking, because if you were not thinking, you would not notice the passage of time. As a matter of fact, far from being boring, the world when looked at without chatter becomes amazingly interesting. The most ordinary sights and sounds and smells, the texture of shadows on the floor in front of you, all these things *are*, without being named and without saying, "That's a shadow, that's red, that's brown, that's somebody's foot." When you do not name things any longer, you start seeing them, because when a person says, "I see a leaf," immediately one thinks of a spearhead-shaped thing outlined in black and filled in with flat green. No leaf looks like that; no, leaves are not green. That is why Lao-tzu said, "The five colors make a man blind; the five tones make a man deaf."

There is another saying that the student who has attained satori goes to hell as straight as an arrow. Anybody who has a spiritual experience, whether one gets it through zazen or through anything that gives you that experience, if you hold onto it, and say, "Now I've got it," in a flash it is gone, out of the window, because the minute you grab a living thing it is like catching a handful of water. The harder you clutch, the faster it squirts through your fingers, and there is nothing to get hold of because you do not need to get hold of anything; you had it from the beginning.

Of course, you can realize this experience through various methods of meditation. The trouble is the people who come out of that experience and brag about it. They say, "I've seen it." Equally intolerable are the people who study Zen and come out and brag to their friends about how long they sat and how much their legs hurt, and what an awful thing it was. The discipline of Zen is not meant to be something awful, and it is not done in a masochistic spirit with the puritanical outlook that suffering is good for you. When I went to school in England the basic premise of education was that suffering builds character, and therefore all senior boys were at liberty to bang about the junior ones with a perfectly clear conscience because they were doing them a favor. It was considered to be good for them because it was building their character. As a result of this kind of attitude the word *discipline* has begun to stink, and it has been stinking for a long time. However we need an entirely new attitude towards this discipline, because without its quiet and non-striving, life becomes messy. When you finally let go, you have to be awfully careful not to melt and become completely liquid, because there is nothing to hold onto.

When you ask most people to lie flat on the floor and relax, you find that they are full of tensions, because they do not really believe that the floor will hold them up, and therefore they are holding themselves. They are uptight and they are afraid that if they do not do this, even though the floor is supporting them, they will suddenly turn into a puddle and trickle away in all directions. On the other hand there are people who, when you tell them to relax, go limp like a rag. Now, the human organism is a subtle combination of hardness and softness, of flesh and bones. The side of Zen which has to do with neither doing or not-doing, but knowing that you are it anyway and you do not have to seek it, that is Zen flesh; but the side in which you can come back into the world with an attitude of not-seeking and knowing you are it and not fall apart, that requires bones. Acquiring Zen bones is one of the most difficult things.

A certain generation we all know about caught onto Zen and started an anything-goes painting, an anything-goes sculpture, and an anything-goes way of life. I think we are recovering from that today. Our painters are beginning once again to return to glory, to marvelous articulateness and vivid color, and nothing like it has been seen since the stained glass of Chartres. That is a good sign, but it requires that there be in our daily life a sense of freedom. I am not just talking about political freedom, I am talking about the freedom which comes when you know that you are it, forever and ever and ever, and it will be so nice when you die, because that will be a change, but it will come back some other way. When you know that, and you have seen through the whole mirage, then watch out, because there may be in you some seeds of hostility, some seeds of pride, some seeds of wanting to put down other people or wanting just to defy the normal arrangements of life. That is why in a Zen monastery, the novices are assigned the light duties and the more senior you get, the heavier your duties. The *rōshi* is, for example, very often the one who cleans out the toilet. There is in this a kind of beautiful, almost princely aestheticism, because by reason of that order being observed all the time, the vast free energy that is contained in the system does not run amok. The understanding of Zen, the understanding of awakening, the understanding of mystical experience, is one of the most dangerous things in the world, and for a person who cannot contain it, it is like putting a million volts through your electric shaver. You blow your mind, and it stays blown.

One who goes off in that way is what is called a *pratyeka-buddha*. He is one who goes off into the transcendental world and is never seen again, and he has made a mistake from the standpoint of Buddhism, because in Buddhism there is no fundamental difference between the transcendental world and this everyday world. The *bodhisattva* does not go off into a *nirvana* and stay there forever and ever; he comes back and lives ordinary everyday life to help other beings to see through it, too. He does not come back because he feels he has some sort of solemn duty to help mankind and all that kind of pious cant. He comes back because he sees that the two worlds are the same, and he sees all other beings as buddhas. To use a phrase of G. K. Chesterton, "But now a great thing in the street seems any human nod, where shift in strange democracy, a million masks of God." It is fantastic to look at people and to see that they really, deep down inside, are enlightened, and they are it; they are faces of the divine.

They look at you, and they say, "Oh no, but I'm not divine, I'm just ordinary little me." And you look at them in a funny way and you see the buddha nature, looking out of their eyes straight at you and saying, it's not I, and saying it quite sincerely. That is why, when you get up against a great guru, the Zen master, he has a funny look in his eye. You say, "I have a problem, guru. I'm really mixed up and I don't understand." Then he looks at you in this queer way, and you think, "Oh dear me, he's reading my most secret thoughts. He is seeing all the awful things I am, all my cowardice, all my shortcomings." He is not doing anything of the kind. He is not even interested in such things.

The bodhisattva, as distinct from the pratyeka-buddha, does not go off into permanent withdrawn ecstasy, and he does not go into a kind of catatonic *samadhi.* That is all right and there are people who can do that because that is their vocation, their specialty. Just as a long thing is the long body of Buddha and a short thing is the short body of Buddha, if you really understand Zen, the Buddhist idea of enlightenment is not comprehended in the idea of the transcendental. It is neither comprehended in the idea of the ordinary, nor in terms of the infinite, nor in terms of the finite, nor in terms of the eternal, nor in terms of the temporal. These are all concepts.

I am not talking about the ordering of ordinary everyday life in a reasonable and methodical way and saying, "If you were nice people, that's what you would do." For heaven's sake, please do not be "nice people." Unless you do have that basic framework of a certain kind of order and a certain kind of discipline, however, the force of liberation will blow the world to pieces; it is too strong a current for the wire.

So then, it is terribly important to see beyond ecstasy. Ecstasy, yes, is the soft and lovely flesh, huggable and kissable, and that is very good. Yet beyond ecstasy are bones, what we call hard facts, the hard facts of everyday life. But we should not forget to mention the soft facts, and there are many of them. The hard fact, the world as seen in an ordinary everyday state of consciousness, however, is really no different from the world of supreme ecstasy. Let us suppose, as so often happens, that you think of ecstasy as insight, as seeing light. There is a Zen poem that says, "A sudden crash of thunder, the mind doors burst open and there sits the ordinary old man."

There is this sudden vision, satori, and the doors of the mind are blown apart and there sits the ordinary old man. Just little old you. Lightning flashes, sparks shower. In one blink of your eyes, you have missed seeing. Why? Because here is the light, the light, every mystic in the world has seen the light, that brilliant blazing energy, brighter than a thousand suns, which is locked up in everything. Now, imagine this: Imagine you are seeing it, like you see aureoles around buddhas, like you see the beatific vision at the end of Dante's *Paradiso*. Vivid, vivid, light so bright that it is like the clear light of the void in the Tibetan *Book of the Dead*, beyond light it is so bright. You watch it receding from you, and on the edges like a great star that becomes a rim of red, and beyond that a rim of orange, yellow, green, blue, indigo, violet, and you see this great *mandala* appearing, this great sun. Beyond the violet there is black, like obsidian, not flat black, but transparent black, like lacquer and again blazing out of the black as the yang comes from the yin there comes sound. There is a sound so tremendous with the white light that you cannot hear it, so piercing that it seems to annihilate the ears. Then, along with the colors, the sound goes down the scale in harmonic intervals, down, down, down, until it gets to a deep thundering bass that is so vibrant, that it turns into something solid, and you begin to get the similar spectrum of textures. Now, all this time you have been watching a kind of a thing radiating out, but it says, "You know, this isn't all I can do," and then rays start going, going, dancing, and naturally the sound starts going, waving, too, as it comes out. Then the textures start varying themselves, and they say, "Well you have been looking at this thing as I have been describing it so far in a flat dimension. Now let's add a third dimension, and it's going to come right at you now." Meanwhile, it says, "It's not that we're just going, going, like this, we're going to do little curlicues, we are going to go round and round like this." Then it says, "Well, that's just a beginning, we can go, here, there, and everywhere, making squares and turns," and then suddenly you see in all the little details that become so intense that all kinds of little subfigures are contained in what you thought were originally the main figures, and the sound starts going, amazing complexities of sound, all over the place, and this thing is going, going, going, and you think you are going to go out of your mind — and suddenly it turns into us, sitting around here.

Thank you very much.

PART FOUR

1968–1969

CHAPTER THIRTEEN

DIVINE ALCHEMY

ALMOST ALL THE GREAT RELIGIONS of the world are, in some way, associated with a drink — Judaism and Christianity with wine, Islam with coffee, Hinduism with the milk of sacred cows, Buddhism with tea. And in one way or another, these sacred drinks are used for sacramental purposes. The sacrament, as it is defined in the Anglican Church, is the outward and visible sign of an inward and spiritual grace. It is a very common feature of religion throughout the world, although one which is highly disapproved of by many people living today in the Western world under the influence of Protestantism and Humanism.

The sacrament, in other words, is a method of giving spiritual power or insight through corporeal means. For example, in the sacrament of baptism, orthodox Christians believe that through the pouring on of water — a physical substance — a person may be in some way united with the grace of God. As another example, some believe that the right words said by the right person over bread and wine transform the bread into the body of Christ and the wine into the blood of Christ. Furthermore, whoever partakes of them — on the principle that you are what you eat — is transformed into Christ.

Behind the more obvious drinks of sacramental liquids associated with the various religions, there are some religions that employ more potent substances. One associates Islam and the whole Arabic culture with the use of hashish. No one who knows anything about the effects of this substance can doubt that the people who painted Persian miniatures and who designed the great arabesques of Islamic civilization had the sort of vision that comes with using hashish.

Likewise, the earliest Vedic texts of India mention something called *soma*. Nobody really knows what soma was, but one may guess, in view of modern practices in India, that it was either a brew derived from cannabis, which today is used by certain types of yogi, or a concoction of psychoactive mushrooms. Shiva worshippers use cannabis widely in the form of *bung*, which is a drink, or *gangia*, which is smoked.

In China, there was for a long time a quest for the elixir of life in the Taoist school of philosophy. This was associated with alchemy, but when you read alchemical texts, you must realize that they are always veiled. The Taoist sages were apparently looking for an elixir of immortality that would convert a human being into an immortal. It was supposed that if you drank the right elixir, when you became an old man, your shriveled skin would peel off and reveal a youth underneath, as a snake changes its skin. We find statues in certain parts of China of venerable old sages with their skin falling off to reveal a young face below, and many sages — indeed even emperors — died from drinking concoctions that purported to be the elixir of life.

One of the ingredients of the elixir was always tea, but of

course tea, as drunk in Buddhist circles, is not the tea that you ordinarily drink. The real ceremonial tea of the Far East is not steeped tea leaves, but green tea ground to a very fine powder. Hot water is poured over it, and then it is stirred with a whisk into a thick mixture. Drinking a few cups of this puts you in a state of extraordinary wakefulness and, therefore, has long been used by Buddhist monks for purposes of meditation. Tea of this sort has a mild psychedelic or consciousness-expanding effect. The Tibetans likewise brew an incredibly thick tea that they mix with yak butter. To us it is an appalling concoction, but to them very soothing and comforting and also wakeful.

Throughout the cultures of Native Americans, religion is centered around divine plants. Native Americans use the peyote cactus, *yagé*, mushrooms such as *Psilocybe mexicana*, the jimsonweed or datura, and a considerable number of other plants that have been catalogued by Professor Schultz of Harvard. Even some seaweeds are considered divine plants. The mushroom *Psilocybe mexicana* is known among certain Native Americans as "the flesh of God."

To an enormous degree, throughout the world, going back as far as we can find any record, there has been the use of some sort of plant — either chewed or distilled or boiled — that transformed consciousness and was alleged to give mankind the vision of divine things. Objection to the use of sacramental plants is strong in the modern West, and there have always been people who deplored this kind of practice. It must be said in the modern West that the use of any material aid to spiritual insight or development is looked upon with disfavor, because it is seen as a crutch. And culture feels happier if it doesn't use a crutch — in other words, if you do it yourself. Somehow or other, the use of a crutch — or as people call it with that question-begging word *drug* — seems to be something that is a sign of weakness. If you are a gutsy fellow and you are going to get this vision in a manner that is natural and legitimate — so that it will really stay with you — you ought to work at it by your own efforts.

You will find this exemplified in Christian Science, a religion that prohibits the use of any medicine for physical health. However, every Christian Scientist is dependent on daily food, both vegetables and meats, and eats them without any feeling of guilt. He ought to realize that if he had sufficient faith, he would be able to live without food or air.

I suppose it sounds far-fetched to say that air is a crutch on which we depend or that the earth is a lamentable ball on which we have to stand in order to hold ourselves up. But if you explore deeply the doctrines and history of almost any religion, you will find that there is simply no do-it-yourself way. Whatever path you follow, invariably you reach a point at which the efforts of your own will or your own ego have to be abandoned.

In Japanese Buddhism, there are two schools: Jiriki and Tariki. *Jiriki* means one's own power. *Tariki* means another's power. Most forms of Buddhism are classified as Jiriki on the principle of the Buddha's final words to his disciples, "Be ye a refuge unto yourselves. Take to yourselves no other refuge, and work out your own deliverance with diligence." And so in Zen and in Tendai, in the Theravadan, or southern forms of Buddhism, you will find that meditation practice or spiritual growth is a matter of using relentless effort to control the mind. But as you concentrate and this effort develops, you reach an impasse in which your will and your ego come to a state of absolute frustration, and you find that there is nothing that you can do to reform yourself, to make yourself unselfish. You discover that, not only is there nothing that you can do, but there is also nothing that you cannot do. In other words, your exerted energy will be as phony as your attempt at relaxation.

At this point in the process of yoga, or meditation, there must transpire a state of surrender, a total giving up. And it is precisely at this moment that the transformation of consciousness, which all these various religions are after, can come about.

In one way or another, all of the religions of the world are concerned with achieving a state of consciousness that is not egocentric, so that we may see through the trick that, during the egocentric state, we always play on ourselves. And the trick that we play on ourselves is that we become unable to be aware of the relativity of opposites. Black and white, light and darkness, good and evil, pleasure and pain, life and death — or even oneself and the external world — in the egocentric state of consciousness seem to be separate and opposed to each other. However, the most elementary logic should tell us that opposites necessarily go together. In other words, if you feel you are a superior person in any way — morally, intellectually, or physically — you have no means of knowing that you're a superior person, except through the presence of relatively inferior people. Were they to disappear you would be left in limbo, and you wouldn't know where you were at all. The higher always depends on the lower in the same way that the flower depends on the soil and the rose on the manure. So, too, the subjective self goes along with the objective, because thoughts are physical events as well as subjective ideas. Everything the self knows is in an inseparable union with the self, but we have managed to screen this out of our normal consciousness and to conduct our lives as if we could make white exist without black, light without darkness, and pleasure without pain.

When the egocentric state is surpassed, it becomes apparent that these things all go together, and the curious consequence of this is that you see the unity of all opposites, that the world is a thing of glory. It is very difficult to explain that transformation logically, but it simply is so with this different kind of consciousness. In other words, everything that you tried formerly to exclude and deny and overcome is seen to be part of a continuous construction, so that the whole world is seen as profoundly harmonious. Everything in it is exactly as it should be.

This is difficult to explain to people who don't see it, and so many people who have this kind of experience remain tongue-tied. Not only is it difficult to explain to ordinary people, but it is very shocking to ordinary people because it seems to undermine all the game rules of the social order. To say that evil things are perfectly all right because they are actually in a secret harmony with good things challenges our ideas of morality. If you are not an intelligent or sensitive person and you understand this idea superficially, you might indeed run amok. This idea could be used to justify any kind of conduct whatsoever on the grounds that everything is part of a universal harmony. This is why, through all the centuries, there has been a kind of esotericism attached to these deep matters.

A kind of secrecy surrounds both the state of consciousness itself and the various means of bringing it about, whether those means are sacramental or some form of meditation, prayer, or other type of spiritual discipline. Let me remind you that there has always been a certain secrecy surrounding this kind of knowledge. Traditionally, these things have not been taught to people or given to people who are inadequately prepared.

This is a grave problem in the modern world, because there are very few secrets in today's world. Scientific knowledge of any kind is public knowledge, at least among scientists. Of course there are types of scientific knowledge that laypeople simply cannot understand because the language in which this knowledge is expressed has to be learned and is difficult to master. Many popularizations of scientific ideas are at least partial falsifications because these ideas cannot be said in English or French or German, even though they may be expressed in algebra. So in a way, all knowledge guards itself, because to understand it you have to follow, to some extent, the path that was followed by the people who discovered it.

Nevertheless, as a result of scientific technology in the modern world, an enormous number of very dangerous things are made available to fools, including fantastic powers of destruction that technology has given us. So it is very difficult indeed to keep secrets in this day and age. Everything has been published, and practically all the mysteries have been let out of the bag. In the view of ancient Hindu philosophers, this would be regarded as a sign of the final decadence of the world and of the coming on of the *Kali-yuga*: the black, destructive epoch at the end of the cycle in which the whole world is destroyed.

Even those religious or spiritual disciplines that believe in an extreme exertion of the will — those Jiriki or self-power disciplines — eventually come to a point that is the same as the Tariki — those that rely on a power outside the individual will that is deeper than the personal ego. Both types of disciplines come to the same place. The difference between the two schools depends on the definition of oneself. If you start out by defining yourself as your ego, then what is the other than you — or a greater power than you — will seem to be different from you. However, if you start out by defining yourself as something more than your ego, then the power that transforms you will still be your own.

For example, most people define their hearts as something other than themselves. We say, "I have a heart," rather than, "I am a heart." For most of us, the heart is an engine that somehow supports the existence of the ego. It is an engine that goes on inside us, like the engine in our car, which — if you're not a mechanic — you don't really understand. You just use it, and so you think of your heart as other than you. It is something that mysteriously happens inside you, but is beyond your control. On the other hand, if you regard your heart as the center of your physical being and very much you, then you become accustomed to thinking that when you beat your heart, you are doing it.

People who come from the Judeo-Christian philosophical traditions are inclined to feel that their heart is not themselves. The Psalmist says, "Behold, I am fearfully and wonderfully made." He looks at his own body and is astounded. And since he does not understand it, it must be the work of a God who is other than himself.

On the other hand, when a Hindu defines himself, he doesn't define himself merely in terms of those types of behavior that are voluntary. He defines himself also in terms of involuntary behavior, and so his heart seems as much himself as anything can be.

So it is really a matter of semantics as to what is self and what is other within you. It depends on where you draw the line. But it seems certain that in all spiritual traditions there comes a point at which the personal ego, the individual will, reaches its limit by one means or another. And at this point it is transformed by something that is not willed, but seems to happen spontaneously. The Christians call it grace. The Hindus call it *prajna*. The Buddhists call it *bodhi*. But in every case, it happens of itself. As the Chinese would say, "It is self-so," so of itself — or spontaneous.

So there are really no grounds for objecting to sacraments. They are something that come to us from the outside and do something to us which is beyond the control — and understanding — of the will. It has always been that way.

However, this is not an experience in which the will and the ego have no part to play. Mystical experience is that transformation of consciousness that produces the sense of union with the divine. However obtained, it is essential that initiates to this experience be grounded — that is, brought down to earth and harmonized with everyday life and human society. This requires discipline, and every tradition looks with disfavor upon those who simply steal the divine secrets and enjoy them without some accompanying kind of discipline. Therefore, the destructive effects of methods used to achieve an altered state of consciousness are particularly problematic for people who have no capacity for the kind of discipline that must go along with their use. This is true not only of sacraments, divine plants, and yoga practices, but all things in which we might find joy. In fact, enjoyment of any kind is really impossible without some sort of an accompanying discipline.

Just think of a few things that are pleasurable and can be simply snatched and swallowed. Start with candy. Would there be such a thing as a palatable candy bar if there were not some expert in the making of sweets? And think of wine. It isn't just alcohol that one throws down. It is a skillfully prepared drink that results from a long tradition of discipline in the vintner's art. Consider racing along in a fast car. You will have an exceedingly short career in this thrilling sport if you don't know how to drive with expertise. And the car itself depends on the skill of a master mechanic.

I cannot think of anything pleasurable that does not require an accompanying discipline — even sex. A lot of people do take sex for granted, and I guess they get a kick out of it. But sex has no profound pleasure unless there is the discipline of an intimate relationship with another human being, which requires a great deal of work and intelligence. The physical aspect of sex is also a considerable art, which very few people ever seem to learn. That is why our culture has sex on the brain. We think about it perpetually. And the reason we are obsessed with sex in a voyeuristic way is because we derive so little satisfaction from it and we exhibit so little discipline and knowledge of how to use it.

So every pleasure involves a method of grounding it and integrating it with everything else. There are ways to attain what is potentially the greatest delight of all: the sense of the divine, the sense of transcending the gulf between the individual and the eternal universe. If you snatch pleasure and experience that pleasure, but you don't do anything with it or you are not properly prepared for it, you are liable to get into trouble. For that reason, psychedelic substances, the chemicals derived from the divine plants, are dangerous. There is no question about it. This is especially true of substances like LSD, which produce their effects as a result of taking an extremely small quantity. If you want to get drunk on beer, you have to put down quite a bit of it, and there is a limit to how much beer one can swallow in an evening. But you don't have that kind of limitation with far more potent substances. The way the Native Americans take peyote cactus makes it pretty difficult to eat. It is nauseating, even though they get used to it. You must chew all that cactus, and so there is a limit to what you can swallow. But with these highly refined elixirs, there is no obvious limit. Our culture is full of downright goofy people who will try anything, even if they don't know anything about it. And the present state of affairs in the United States regarding the whole matter of psychedelic substances is in such confusion, it defies description.

These substances are called drugs, but this is a word that is not clearly defined. There is no obvious line that can be drawn between a drug and something used for food, like vitamins. A group of physicians and a group of lawyers got together not so long ago to see if they could arrive at a legal definition of addiction — that is to say, dependence on some chemical. They kept finding that whenever they thought they were close to the definition, their definition could also be applied to dependence on a foodstuff. So, this is a very difficult thing to define.

There are wide differences between various types of chemicals that produce changes in consciousness. All of them could be said to be addictive in a least a psychological sense. For example, suppose you belong to an in-group where taking LSD is *de rigeur*, and you know it is the thing to do. Soon everybody in the group is comparing notes as to how often and how much they take. You engage in this one-upmanship. This is asinine because it proves that you are following the practice simply to remain in the in-group. If you had disciplined yourself in the use of consciousness transformation, you would have soon come to see the folly of belonging to an in-group. And this is only one of many examples of how individuals and groups of people become psychologically dependent on drugs.

Other substances are addictive in a much more physical sense. Opiates, for example, cause very difficult withdrawal symptoms if one doesn't use them constantly. However, this addictive factor is not characteristic of most substances used for this purpose. In other words, most substances used for the expansion of consciousness are not narcotic. The word *narcotic* means sleep-inducing or soporific, and narcotics dull or dim the senses. Alcohol, in sufficient quantity, is a narcotic. Opium, likewise, is a narcotic. It is used for dulling the sense of pain, and its derivative, morphine, is a narcotic in the strictest sense of the word.

However, substances such as mescaline, which is the derivative of peyote or a chemical synthesis of peyote, is not a narcotic. LSD is not a narcotic. Psilocybin from the mushroom is not a narcotic, and cannabis is not a narcotic. These substances tend to do something very different from producing sleep. They tend, instead, to produce a peculiar kind of wakefulness and a sharpening rather than a dimming of consciousness. So they must not be lumped in the same category as true narcotics.

Narcotics are also addictive. Alcohol is addictive, and the opiates are addictive. One can become physically dependent on them, and only with great difficulty can one shake them off. The same is true of tobacco. It is very difficult for a hardened smoker to drop the habit. I doubt, however, that tobacco is actually a narcotic in the sense of being sleep-inducing.

Our absurdly paranoid government agencies have not learned in fifty years the difference between narcotics and nonarcotic drugs. Nor have they learned how to handle these problems. Despite the lessons of prohibition, the authorities still think that the only way to deal with dangerous narcotics is simply to suppress them, not realizing that this makes them all the more attractive. It also creates an enormous crime problem, which, without the suppression of drugs, would not exist. It is very difficult to suppress these things completely. You can suppress them a little bit, and you can pick out a few fall guys and make terrible examples of them by putting them in prison for an incredible number of years, but this only scratches the surface. When something illegal is really popular, there is no way to suppress it because all the hotels in the United States would not be sufficient to jail all the criminals involved. This approach has never worked. Why people don't learn from history is beyond my comprehension.

As people become aware that there are an enormous number of varieties of things that will produce psychedelic effects, the problem becomes much worse. In particular, such substances as LSD can be compressed into such small volumes that their detection is virtually impossible. So the moment these substances become a racket — something from which organized crime can make a good profit — the possibilities of manipulating the market become enormous. The real racket is the suppression of drugs. We have never really understood what control is, and we don't see the difference between controlling oneself and strangling oneself. In other words, a person who is a controlled automobile driver is certainly not a person who has no car or keeps his car locked in the garage. A very controlled dancer is certainly not a person who never dances. The control of things is not the suppression of them, but their use in a sensible and proper way. And this has not penetrated the consciousness of our authorities.

You cannot suppress mankind's fascination and curiosity about states of consciousness other than the normal. These things are eternally fascinating to human beings, and will always be pursued. Whether you think it is good or bad makes no difference. It will be done. At the present time, for example, if people want to experiment with LSD or mescaline or any consciousness-changing material, they are in a ridiculous situation. They cannot even pay a psychiatrist to sit with them and take care of them while they do it, because that would be illegal. What they will do is *not* have a psychiatrist or experienced person present. They will try it out all on their own without any preparation and endanger themselves, because drugs, under unfavorable circumstances and when used by people who do not have good psychic balance, can bring about prolonged bouts of psychosis. With these substances, this can lead to a good deal of trouble. But the difficulty is that we are, as a culture, not prepared for the controlled use of these substances. That is why there is a panic and why our current method of dealing with drugs is probably worse than allowing them to circulate freely.

I would not for one moment advocate the free circulation of these substances so that anybody could go into a drugstore and buy them. But I think it would be better than total suppression because it is less destructive. But what we don't know is how to apply proper controls to the transformation of human consciousness by relatively easy means because we are not clear as to the role of these chemicals or the proper role of the physician. And this is something I want to consider.

In ancient times, there was no clear distinction between priests and physicians. An individual might be primarily a priest and secondarily a physician. Over time, the functions of priest and physician began to separate. The advent of scientific medicine was opposed by the Church, and therefore priests tended not to practice scientific medicine. The practitioners of scientific medicine, being other than priests, separated from religious professions. As medicine developed in the West, the deep concern of the physician became to preserve people from death — to be a healer — and the function of looking after death was abandoned to the priest and the minister. So when the doctor, in treating a patient, gives up hope of saving that life, he is out of his role. He doesn't know what to do beyond that point, and therefore the priest is summoned.

So the work of a doctor is curative throughout. He is, in all his activities, opposed to death and regards death as the enemy. This is, of course, not true of every individual physician. But it is true of medical ethics and of physicians generally. This means that people with terminal illnesses are being tortured — albeit with a good motive, but nonetheless tortured — by being kept alive in a state of near mummification. We have come to believe that while there is life, there is hope, and that in the next few days there might be some amazing medical discovery that could cure the terminally ill. It would be a shame to let them die and not reap the benefit of such a cure. And yes, there always might be.

So the fact that the physician is, in general, out of his role and does not know what to do in the face of death has a very important connection with another aspect of the physician's trade: He does not know what to do with chemicals or drugs that do not have the function of healing a physical disease. In a way, all consciousness-expanding drugs have something to do with death because, as Jung pointed out, all spiritual disciplines are preparations for death.

Every spiritual discipline involves a form of death — what is called "dying to oneself" or what the Christians call "dying daily" — and this is identified with the crucifixion of St. Paul. In the famous words of St. Paul, "I am crucified with Christ, yet I live. But not I, for it is Christ that lives in me." He also uses the phrase "being baptized into Christ's death." That's all very funny language to the modern mind. But it is a commonplace of the spiritual disciplines that what you must do is die in the midst of life. You are born again a second time, and that death refers to the death of the ego.

You live behind the state of consciousness in which you thought you were no more than an isolated, individual center of consciousness. That perspective drops back, and in that sense you have died.

As an aid to that, spiritual disciplines often involve the contemplation of death. We think it is rather ghoulish nowadays, but monks used to keep skulls on their desks, and Buddhists meditate in graveyards. Hindu yogis meditate beside the burning funeral pyres on the banks of the Ganges, where they are always confronted with death, knowing this is going to happen to them.

Gurdjieff once said, "If anything would possibly save mankind from its idiocy, it would be the clearest possible recognition by every individual that he, and all others around him, are most certainly going to die." When this thought becomes perfectly clear to you, surprisingly it becomes a source of intense joy and vitality. When you have accepted your own death in the midst of life, it means that you have let go of yourself, and you are therefore free. You are no longer plagued by worry and anxiety. You know that you are done for anyhow, so there is no need to fight constantly to protect yourself. What's the point? And it isn't just that people spend all their time doing something to really protect themselves, like taking out an insurance policy or eating properly. Instead it is what we do that doesn't cause any action at all: the constant inner worry that leads to no action except more worry. That is what is given up by a person who really knows that they are dead. So do you see that transcending yourself, going beyond your ego, is the great preparation for death?

Now, if the medical profession takes the side of the ego against death — opposes death and regards death as the supreme evil — then the doctor really is out of his role at the bedside of a dying patient. And he also is out of his role when it comes to handling drugs that are not designed to heal sicknesses as we ordinarily define them.

But what really happens when someone develops a state of mind not considered to be psychologically normal? Sometimes a priest is called. But today, very few people, even churchgoing Christians, take priests seriously. When somebody in a good Christian family shows signs of mental derangement, the priest is very seldom called in. One calls in a psychiatrist. Why? Because he is a scientist, and, in our culture, the scientist has a greater reputation for magical power than do priests or ministers. We only call in the priest when all hope is abandoned.

Catholic or Anglican priests, by and large, are very used to handling death. They know what to do, and they come without any embarrassment, with the book open to the right place, and proceed to administer the last rites. And that is rather good, because here is a man who knows what to do and isn't flustered in the face of death. That in itself has a calming influence. However, a lot of people feel that this isn't really the way to handle death because they don't understand these last rites. So if the priest is called in only in desperation, this suggests that he does not have much power anyway. He may have power to do something with the Lord and the world beyond, but it is very doubtful he will be effective in this world.

Under such circumstances, both priest and physician need to

take another look at death and rediscover the all-important fact that life without death has no value. Death, as Norman Brown pointed out in his book *Life Against Death*, "is what confers individuality upon us." It is your limits in time that constitute you, just as much as your limits in space. Death therefore always overshadows the whole of life, and life would have no meaning, no point, if it didn't have death to balance it. Life and death are the in-breath and out-breath, the coming and going, the rising and falling. They are mutually interdependent. Death is a very important and valuable thing that has been swept under the carpet.

So then, in a culture where priest and physician have become widely separated, the sudden bursting upon us of sacramental substances is an embarrassment to both. It is embarrassing to the priest for many reasons. Suppose we were to say that psychedelic substances are not the province of physicians and psychiatrists, but the province of the clergy. Everybody would throw up their hands and say, "These people have no scientific training. They don't know anything about neurology. They don't know anything about the subtle effects of these things on the human organism. How could they be responsible?" And, alas, that is true. The clergy have no training in neurology — so much the worse for them.

On the other hand, the psychiatrist and neurologist, with very few exceptions, have had no training in theology. And when most of them talk about theology, they reveal their abysmal ignorance of the whole matter.

So the issue falls right between the two schools. Although there are talented individuals who understand this sort of thing, there is no recognized class of people who might be called, for example, theo-botanists or theo-neurologists. We need to see the development of such a profession. Until we have it, we will be in a difficult situation.

How to deal with drugs, if you will, or chemicals that do not seem to have, as their primary use, the healing of a physical disease, poses an interesting problem. There is a sense in which these substances are medicine, rather than diet. A medicine is something you need when something is out of order, whereas a diet is what you live on permanently. (Of course, corrections in diet can have a medicinal effect.)

But surely there is a very true sense in which we can say that a world based on an egocentric consciousness is very seriously sick. Everybody knows why, and we can see all around us that we are stark raving mad and are preparing to destroy ourselves. This is a sickness that needs some kind of remedy — maybe even a desperate remedy. The use of substances that would lift us out of the egocentric situation could therefore be considered medicine for a social disorder.

But again, I would say that substances used in that way should be used as medicine in the sense that they should not become diet. In this matter, everybody speaks for himself, but I have discovered that this is not the sort of thing you take very often, as you might go to church. It is something that you can take several times in gradually diminishing quantity. Beyond that, it is up to you to integrate your vision with everyday life.

However, there are other people who seem to think that the great thing to do is to start out with a little and then keep on going, making it bigger and bigger, as if they were looking for something that should lie at the end of the line. But then it becomes a diet, and that is getting hooked on medicine. Very rightly doctors don't like to hook you on medicine because the goal of a good doctor is to get rid of you as a chronic patient. He doesn't want people hanging on to him and always coming for help. He wants to set you back on your own feet, and that is an excellent principle.

So the doctor has something to say to the priest because priests tend, by and large, to want to keep you coming to church so that you will pay your dues and the Church will prosper. So the more people they can get hooked on religion, the better. Now priests ought to learn from doctors and try to get rid of people by telling them their gospel, or whatever it is they have to say, and then saying, "Now you've had it, go away." If the priest did that, he would create a vacuum, and it would always be filled. The faster a doctor can get people out of his office, the sooner they go around and tell everybody, "This man cured me. I didn't have to go back." And the more people will come in. There are always plenty of sick people. So in the same way, the religious man ought to handle a huge turnover of people coming through and going away. Then he is really working.

But he should not get them hooked on the medicine of churches. There is a Latin expression that means "the Cross is the medicine of the world." But people get hung up on the cross. Jesus didn't get hung up. According to the Christian mythology, Jesus came alive again afterwards, if only for a while. In the same way, if Christians really believed in the inner meaning of the doctrine, they wouldn't get hung up on the cross either, but embrace it only temporarily. "I am crucified with Christ, nevertheless I live."

So also, when it comes to the use of any technique whatsoever for spiritual awakening, whether it is yoga or LSD or religion, there is something to be learned from Buddha's symbol of the raft. The Buddha likened his method — his *dharma*, or doctrine — to a raft. This method is also called a *yana*, or vehicle — hence the *Mahayana*, or big vehicle, and the *Hinayana*, or little vehicle. The raft takes you across the river: This shore is birth and death, and the other shore is liberation, or nirvana. You climb aboard the raft to cross the river. But when you get to the other shore, you leave the raft behind.

In much the same way, Zen Buddhism uses a technique: the *kōan*, or meditation problem. It is like knocking at a door with a brick. When the door is opened, you don't carry the brick inside. You leave the brick behind.

Each of these techniques is a means, *upaya*, and each has as its objective the deliverance from the means. The Christian mystics speak of the highest state of contemplative prayer, or union with God, as a union without means. And I would extend the sense of the word *means* even to ecstasy. In other words, in the great religious traditions, ecstasy is not a final state. For example, in Zen, when the experience of satori, or awakening, comes about, there is a feeling of ecstasy. You feel as if you were walking on air, and you feel absolutely unobstructed. You feel as happy as a lark, and it is marvelous. But that in itself is only incidental.

A Zen proverb says, "A monk who has a satori goes to hell as straight as an arrow." In other words, to have it is to cling to it, and although you may think that the ecstasy is the important thing, it isn't. Ecstasy is an intermediate stage to bring you back to the point where you can see that everyday life — your ordinary mind, as they say in Zen — is the Buddha mind. Everyday life, just as it is, is the great thing, and there is no difference between that and the divine life.

However, so long as you think that there is a state of affairs in which you can say of the big thing — whether it is God, nirvana, Brahma, the Divine, or the Tao — "I've got it," you haven't. The moment you regard it as some sort of object, as some sort of state or some sort of thing that you can possess, you have pushed it away from yourself. The one thing you can't lay your hands on is you. You would never figure it out, not in a million years, and you can't even find out who it is that wants to find out. And whoever wants to find out who it is and wants to find out, will never get at it. That's the thing. It is the thing that is most close to you, as Francis Thompson said, "Nearer is he than breathing, closer than hands and feet."

What is absolutely central to you is that which you can never make an object of knowledge, and so you finally get to the point that you don't have to have anything, because you are it. You don't even need to insist that you are it, because if you have to insist on that, then you doubt it, and you will have to go around saying to yourself, "Be still and know that I am God." But that's for beginners. When you really get at the end of it, there isn't a trace. No means are left, no methods, no getting hold if it. No meditation, no LSD — no nothing — because it is just the way it is.

To sum up: In the final analysis, all spiritual awakenings involve something beyond the will and the ego. You cannot do it yourself, so it makes little difference what you use to get there. Some ways are easier than others. It's easier to use theo-botany, a divine plant, than to bang your head against a brick wall. But with the very ease of it, there is the danger that you may neglect the discipline that must go with it. With "banging your head against a brick wall," at least you are sure to know the danger before anything happens. The discipline is relatively easy to handle. Of course, as Aldous Huxley once said, "To insist upon using the more arduous ways to attain the mystical state, is rather like burning down your farm house every time you want roast pork." The problem for us is that we don't have someone who integrates the role of priest and the role of physician, and the division into two roles has left both impoverished. So there is nobody who is really competent to deal with death or with preparation for death, and that creates a problem for us.

Finally, let me remind you that the most subtle danger in all these things — yoga or chemical methods — is fixation on ecstasy and not knowing how to go beyond ecstasy and beyond looking at the divine as something that one can personally possess.

CHAPTER FOURTEEN

DEMOCRACY IN THE
KINGDOM OF HEAVEN

THE GREAT DISCUSSION GOING ON in what we call the new theology is the revolution within standard-based Christianity. For years and years the clergy — the ministry of the various churches such as Episcopalian, Methodist, Baptist, Congregational, Unitarian, even in some cases Disciples of Christ and Lutheran — have been discussing religion in their theological seminaries in terms so utterly different from what you normally hear from the pulpit. Every graduate of an intelligent theological school has a sense of intense frustration as they go out to work in a community or parish church. This is because they do not believe in what they are supposed to preach. And this has, in a way, been true for a long, long time.

Clergy, except in the Roman Catholic Church where the situation is somewhat different, are very heavily controlled by the laity because he who pays the piper calls the tune. Therefore they are in a state of constant frustration because those who contribute most heavily, and therefore are most interested in the church, tend to be conservative people. They want that old-time religion, although as a matter of fact, what they call the old-time religion is really quite modern. But that is what they want.

In the British army they have a thing called church parade. There is a famous story about a drill sergeant who would get all the troops up for church parade on a Sunday morning, and then he would call out, "Catholics to the right, Protestants to the left, fancy religions in the middle." To the degree that intelligent people in our culture have any religion at all, it tends to be a fancy religion, one of the new kinds such as Unity, Christian Science, Theosophy, Buddhism, Vedanta, or some kind of special Protestant offshoot such as the Fellowship Church in San Francisco or the Community Church in New York, that are very liberal, very left-wing theologically.

The new theology has emerged at this time because to a very large extent, the clergy are fed up. Christianity has its back to the wall, and the Pope knows this better than anybody. So hand in hand with this ecumenical movement there comes a reconsideration of what on earth Christianity is all about. Is there *one* God? Is there a God at all? A lot of people are boldly saying all ideas of God are to be abandoned.

As an English priest by the name of Father Mascal put it, the basic assumption of the secularist movement in Christian theology is that life is a journey between the maternity ward and the crematorium. That is all there is; that's it. That is the only life the Christian religion has to encounter. Therefore, with this abandonment of God, and even the idea that the universe is supernaturally controlled, the Christian religion fastens itself with peculiar and increased fervor to the figure of Jesus of Nazareth. As one wit put it, there is no God, and Jesus Christ is His only son.

There is something strange about Christianity. It shares with Islam and Judaism what we might call theological imperialism.

Christians of even the most liberal stripe fervently believe that their religion is the best religion. They say, "Jesus Christ is the only Son of God." That isn't really an orthodox way of saying it, but it is the way orthodox people do say it. Otherwise they say, "Jesus is the greatest man who ever lived." The point is that you make a commitment to the following of Jesus as an historical personage. And for some reason or other, people who commit themselves to this exclusive kind of following of Jesus become exceedingly obstreperous. They will either damn other religions outright or, far more insidious, damn them with faint praise. "Old Buddha taught some very good things, and we all are indebted to his great moral principles." But there always follows a pitch for the sole following of Jesus as the Lord and Master, head and shoulders above all.

The trouble with that has always been that when you get into a theological argument with a person who is this kind of Christian, you find yourself in a situation where the advocate and the judge are the same person. That is to say, Jesus is found to be the best man in the world by the standards of Christianity, because those are the standards with which this kind of person judges. Therefore, you will find that people who leap to these judgments usually do not know very much about any other kind of religion. The courses on comparative religion in theological schools are shockingly superficial and grossly inaccurate. This is coming to the front now. The real purpose of belonging to a church is to be saved, and being saved means belonging to the most "in" group. You have to be part of a select group if you want to know who you are, to distinguish yourself, because then you know you are different from the people who are not part of your group. There you get a contrast. This is the basic arrangement for a church. If you want to be in some kind of an insider's group, you must put everybody else beyond the pale.

St. Thomas Aquinas actually gave the show away when he said

that the blessed in heaven will often walk to the battlements and look down and delight in the justice of God being properly carried out in hell. But you may be very liberal, you may not believe in hell. After all, it is not nice or sophisticated nowadays to believe in everlasting damnation. So we have new phrases for it, such as "failing to be a real person," "sinking below the human level," or "entering into final and irremediable psychosis." All of these are new phrases for either damnation or heresy. So you can know you are saved only if you know that somebody else is not. It is very difficult to imagine a state of affairs wherein everyone and everything is saved. You have to be a mystic even to think about that, because it requires a state of consciousness that transcends oppositions, and you cannot do that with ordinary logic. You have to have a new kind of logic, the kind I am using at the moment when I point out that damned people and saved people need each other. They are in a symbiotic relationship. They go together in the same way as the back and front of something do, because if something has a front it has to have a back too. And so the very fact that fronts and backs go together indicates that there is a unity between opposites, even such apparent opposites as the damned and the saved.

It is only as you begin to realize you need the damned people in order to be saved, and they need the saved in order to be damned, that you can start laughing about it. And of course that laughter is very subversive. You know the rules: you are not supposed to laugh in church, or in courts of law, either. They are places where laughter makes people nervous, because laughter is supposed to be a sign of disrespect. However, that may not be so at all. Dante said that the song of the angels in paradise sounded like the laughter of the universe. But in church — especially in the more serious kind — laughing is very bad form. Why? Because if you look at the design of a Catholic church you will notice it is based on the design of the courtroom of a king. If you look at a Protestant church you will see that it is based upon the design of a law court. Indeed, the Protestant minister wears exactly the same robes as an American judge, and all those pews and boxlike stalls are the same as you will find in the old-fashioned court with the witness box and jury box. This is the original idea of the Christian church.

An ancient Roman church is called a basilica. That means the courtroom of a king, or the throne room. The altar is the throne of God, but in a courtroom the king is very nervous, because anybody who takes it on himself to govern other people and rule must always watch out. Therefore he always had his back to the wall, and he is flanked by attending guards and high ministers of state. Just so that nobody will get up and make trouble, he has them either on their knees or flat on their faces when they are in his presence. And, of course, no one must laugh. That would be laughing at Mr. Big.

This was the pattern or the model on which the Judeo-Christian idea of God was based, and it is a political model. The titles for God — King of Kings, Lord of Lords — were taken from those of the supreme emperors of Persia. So at morning prayer in the English church the clergyman gets up and says, "Almighty and everlasting God, the only ruler of princes, King of Kings, Lord of Lords, who dost from thy throne behold all dwellers on earth, most graciously deign to behold our gracious sovereign lady Queen Elizabeth and all the royal family." You may not believe literally that God sits on a throne, or even has a body to put on one, or that He wears a crown, or that He has a beard, but that image still colors your feeling about the character of God. Images are more powerful than intellectual concepts.

You may know that it says in the prayer book that God is a spirit without a body or passions, omnipresent to all places, and eternal to all time. Therefore one thinks, as Hegel does, of the gaseous vertebrate, or else of an enormously diffused sea of luminous Jell-O filling all time and space. Everybody uses images. But behind those images are the old images that influenced us in childhood. If you still attend church and use that imagery, emotionally you still feel toward God as you would if you took it literally. This political model of God has dominated the West. The world is related to God as subjects are to a king, or as artifacts are to their maker. We have a ceramic model of the universe, because it is said in the Book of Genesis that God made Adam out of the dust of the ground. In other words, He made a clay figure and blew the breath of life into the nostrils of the figurine and it came to life.

The Hindus do not have to cope with this model of the universe because they do not see the universe as God's creation — in the sense of being an artifact — they see it as God's drama. They see the world as active, not created. God is that which is pretending to be all that is. Everybody is really God, a mask of God, who is playing that He is you. But He is doing it so well that He has taken himself in. He is both the audience and the actor. He wants to get you crying. He wants to get you sitting on the edge of your seat in anticipation. God, the ultimate actor, has convinced himself completely that the act is real.

The Chinese have a third model. Theirs is of an organic universe, a great organism. It is alive; it grows. It is an intelligent order.

Those are the three great models of the world. When, a long time ago, the West stopped believing seriously in God, we Westerners still retained the idea of the world as an artifact, we merely graduated from a ceramic model of the universe to a fully automatic, mechanical model, which is now common sense for most people living today.

I return to the point that the clergy and people of the Church do not really believe at all in God in the old-fashioned sense of the word. If they did seriously believe the Christian religion in its orthodox form, they would be screaming in the street. But even the Jehovah's Witnesses are more or less polite when they come and call at your house. If they really believed that you were going to hell, they would make a bigger fuss about you than they would if you had the bubonic plague. But nobody really takes Christianity seriously anymore, because they do not believe in it. They know they ought to believe in it. In fact many sermons are exhortations to have more faith, which means that we all recognize that we do not really believe it, but we ought to. We feel very guilty about it, but we do not have the moral strength to believe in this. However, it is not only a matter of moral strength. It is a matter of being asked to believe in something that most people feel is nonsense, which is that the world is run on the lines of a state. How can you be a citizen of the United States, having taken an oath that a republican form of government is the best form of government, and believe that the universe is a monarchy?

Intelligent people have always realized that this political model for the cosmos will not do. Actually, no serious theologian ever did believe that God was an old gentleman with whiskers sitting on a golden throne. Never. The bishop of Woolwich says in his book *Honest to God* that there is not that sort of a someone out there. He is very naive in a way. He could have taken huge quotations out of St. Thomas Aquinas, out of the great fathers of the Church, from Origen, from Clement of Alexandria, from St. Gregory Nazianzen, from St. John of Damascus, from St. Basil the Great, from St. Augustine, from St. Ambrose, from Bernard of Clairvaux, and Albert the Great; he could have quoted all those perfectly orthodox, very correct theologians and shown that they never believed in a God with whiskers. He could have come forward and said, "See, this is a perfectly orthodox book, and I am not a revolutionary. I am just going back to the real old-time religion." He did not do that, and do you know why? He told me. He had never read those writers in theological school. His religious training was entirely confined to biblical studies, and never got that far.

It is the same with ever so many people. One of the reasons so many people turn to an Oriental religion is that the intellectual level at which Oriental religions were first presented in the West was so much higher than the intellectual level at which Christianity was presented in the local church. If you lived in India, or Ceylon, of course you would attend the local Buddhist monastery, and its sermons would be just as junky as the stuff taught at our local churches. They do not tell the people about things like the great void, or how to practice meditation — that is for specialists. All they care about is gaining merit, earning better circumstances in your next life, or getting out of evil karma. That is what popular Buddhism is really about. The trouble in the West is that everybody is becoming educated, and there is a terrific degree of literacy. Therefore the public has to be treated with respect. You cannot say "the public be damned" anymore. There are too many educated people.

I would say the God that really is dead is this politically modeled God, however conceived. The divine paternalistic authority who rules the universe — to whom you as an ego are related, by analogy, as a subject is to a king — is just not holding up. But what are the alternatives for Western people with a Christian background? What other kind of God could we have? One of the possibilities is no God at all. This is what people on the far left of the new theology are saying. A man like James Pike, on the other hand, is on the new theology's right wing. He very definitely believes in God — he is a theist — but he does not believe in anything with whiskers on it, nor does he really believe in the political model.

We must choose, then, between a mechanical universe that is no more than it appears to be, and a very refined conception of a God that would be called "It" instead of "He." It makes a very powerful difference which pronoun you use. Even "He-She," as the Christian Scientists talk about the "father-mother," is sort of complicated. "It" is rather simple. But then when you say "it," does this mean that God is like electricity that does not seem to have any independent intelligence of its own, but is just energy, something that goes "zoom"? Is God, as an "it," something like that?

The funny thing is it is very difficult to be a real atheist. In 1928 in the houses of parliament in England, the Church of England wanted a new revised prayer book. However, because the church and the state are inseparable in England, the houses of parliament had to vote on whether the new prayer book might be used. Somebody got up and said, "It is perfectly ridiculous that an assemblage which contains a number of atheists should vote on the inner politics of the Church of England." But another member got up and said, "I don't think there are any atheists here, not really. We all believe in some sort of something somewhere."

Now in the theological world, it just doesn't do to believe in "some sort of something somewhere," because one thing that theologians detest is vagueness. Even no God at all is preferred to vagueness, because at least atheism is clear and precise. You should hear what they say. "No beating around the bush old man. You know it is just fuzzy thinking to believe in a great universal mind that is an undifferentiated aesthetic continuum, and that is all there is to 'some sort of something somewhere.' This is woolly thinking. Either give us no God, or else give us a God with a definite character and a clear moral will and precise standards who will not be pushed around, a God with biblical quality."

What do you do? Do you separate your mind into two different compartments, in one of which you keep abreast of science and the modern world, while in the other you simply have nothing to do with all that? To combine those two compartments would make very difficult the possibility of belief in the ludicrous propositions that are usually called religion. But a lot of people want a religion that is difficult to believe in because they feel that difficult beliefs are a kind of test of faith.

So there is a possibility of that kind of God, and there is also the possibility of no God. Is life just this trip from the maternity ward to the crematorium, and is the purpose of religion just the improvement of that trip? That is to say, is the whole business of religion to get rid of poverty and war and exploitation and disease, or is there something else? Those who take the view that there is nothing else, which we will call the secular position of theology, are of course strongly influenced by contemporary philosophy — especially in that form that is called scientific empiricism or logical positivism — which maintains that the idea of God is not a fallacy, but is a meaningless idea. In other words, they maintain that the propositions that God exists, and that God is the origin and creator and governor of everything that is happening are utterly devoid of meaning. It is to them as if one were to say, "Everything is up." They maintain that no logical proposition whatsoever can be made about all propositions because all propositions are labels on boxes and you cannot have the box containing all boxes, because this box would have no outside, and therefore it would not be a box. All propositions, all words, must refer to classes of some kind, and you cannot have the class of all classes.

Secularists also say that the notion of a God is meaningless on the grounds that it does not help you to make any predictions. Or they ask, What evidence would completely satisfy you as disproving the existence of God? And no believer in God can think of any evidence that would conclusively prove that there isn't a God. Similarly, psychoanalysts are completely incapable of thinking of any evidence that would disprove the existence of the Oedipus complex. So on logical grounds contemporary philosophers take the position that the idea of God is a meaningless idea. And since many theologians are influenced by modern philosophy, they take these arguments seriously and would like to secularize the whole conception of religion or, to put it in Bonhoeffer's words, "Have Christianity without religion."

When I hear someone say that there is nothing to life except the trip between the maternity ward and the crematorium, I recall having heard something like that before. When asked, "What is the Buddha?" a Chinese master replied, "It's windy again this morning." Another Buddhist master, on his deathbed, wrote the poem, "From the bathtub to the bathtub I have uttered stuff and nonsense." This is the bathtub in which the baby is washed at birth and the bathtub in which the corpse is washed before burial. "All the time in between," he said, "I was going yakety-yak." Now, do those poems mean what they say? Not quite. They are based on a life devoted to the discipline of a very particular kind of meditation that culminates in a completely shattering experience, which is very difficult to talk about. Generally speaking, it is the encounter with eternity, with the eternal — not necessarily in the sense of that which goes on and on through time, but the eternal as the timeless that transcends time and is beyond measurement in terms of hours and days. When a person who is in that state of consciousness, or has been through it, looks at the ordinary, everyday world, he sees the ordinary, everyday world as we see it, but with a very extraordinary difference. If we have to put that difference into some sort of Western, Christian-influenced language, he would perhaps say, "Don't you realize that sitting around here in this room, with our ordinary, everyday faces and clothes and personalities, we are sitting smack in the middle of the beatific vision? This sitting here in this room is precisely infinity and eternity. It is it. This is the beatific vision. This is God."

In this meditation religion, they still have temples, they still have buddhas, and they still chant sutras and offer incense and ring gongs and all that kind of thing, but they also say that to really get to the highest level of religion you have to kill the Buddha.

Supposing a clergyman got up one day in the pulpit and said, "Every time you say Jesus Christ, you have to wash out your mouth." Or, "If you meet God the Father, kill Him. If you meet God the Son, kill Him. If you meet God the Holy Spirit, kill It. If you meet St. Augustine, kill him. Kill them all right away." This is simply translating into Christian terms what a Buddhist teacher said in about the year A.D. 800.

However, I do not think this "killing Buddha" is what is happening in the new theology. I think they are just getting rid of God.

We are supposed to believe in the Ten Commandments, and one of them says, "Thou shalt not make to thyself any graven image of anything that is in heaven above, or the earth beneath, nor bow down, nor worship them." What I have been talking about — this killing of Buddha — is a destruction of idols, because the most dangerous graven images are not those that are made of wood and stone, they are those that are made of ideas. It is well known to the great mystical traditions all over the world that the supreme vision can only come when you have rid your mind of every idea of God whatsoever. It would be like cleaning a window on which somebody has painted blue sky. To see the true sky you have to scrape off the paint. You may say, "My goodness, you shouldn't take that nice blue painting off. It was done by a great artist. See how pretty the clouds are. You mustn't do that because we won't have any of the blue sky anymore." But the great mystics have always ceased to cling to God, because the only God you can cling to is the idea of God.

In order to discover God you have to stop clinging entirely. Why does one cling to God? For safety, of course. You want to save something; you want to save yourself. I don't care what you mean by saved, whether it means just feeling happy, or that life is meaningful, or that there is somebody up there who cares. If you do not cling to one god, you cling to another: the state, money, sex, yourself, power. These are all false gods. But there has to come a time when clinging stops; only then does the time of faith begin. People who hold onto God do not have any faith at all, because real faith lies in not holding onto anything.

In the Christian tradition this nonclinging is called the cloud of unknowing. There is a book about it written by a fourteenth-century British monk. He got it from a man called Dionysius the Areopagite, who had assumed the name of St. Paul's Athenian convert, a Syrian monk living in the sixth century. Meister Eckhart, St. Thomas Aquinas, John Scotus Erigena, and many other great medieval theologians studied Dionysius the Areopagite. His book was *The Theologica Mystica*, in which he explained that, in order to come to full union with God, you must give up every conception of God whatsoever. And he enumerates the concepts that must be given up: don't think that God is a oneness or a threeness or a unity or a spirit or any kind of anything that the human mind can conceive. He is beyond all that.

This is called apophatic theology, a Greek term that contrasts with cataphatic. When you speak catiphatically you say what God is like. Dionysius also wrote a book of cataphatic theology called *The Divine Names*. Cataphatic theology tells what God is like according to analogy. He is like a father. We do not say God is a cosmic male parent but that he is, in some respect, like a father. This is the cataphatic method. The apophatic method says what God is not. All those theologians who followed Dionysius said that the highest way of talking about God is in negative terms, just as, to use Dionysius's own image, when a sculptor makes a figure he does it entirely by removing stone, by taking away. In that same spirit, St. Thomas Aquinas said, "Because God, by His infinity, exceeds every idea to which the human mind can reach, the best way to speak of Him is by removal." That is, removing from our view of God every inadequate concept. This is what the Hindus refer to as *neti neti*, saying of the Brahman of the supreme reality, "It is not this, it is not this."

This intellectual operation of destroying concepts must go hand in hand with the psychological operation of ceasing to cling to any image whatsoever. Simply cease to cling, because there is no need to. There is no need to cling because when you are born you were kicked off a precipice. There was a big explosion, and you are falling, and a lot of other things are falling with you, including some pretty large lumps of rock, of which one is called the earth. It will not help you to cling to the rocks, when they are falling, too. It may give you an illusion of safety, but everything is falling, and falling apart. The ancients said, in the words of Heracleitus, "All is transient, all flows." You cannot cling to anything; it is like grabbing at smoke with a nonexistent hand. Clinging only makes people anxious.

When you come to the realization that you cannot cling to anything, that there is nothing to cling to, there transpires a change of consciousness that we can call either faith or letting go. In Sanksrit they put it this way: *tat tvam asi*, meaning literally "Thou are thou," or as we would say, "You are it." And if you are God, then you cannot have an idea of God any more than you can chew your own teeth. You do not need any idea of God. The sun does not need to shine on itself. Knives do not need to cut themselves. All the things you see on the outside are states of the nervous system in the brain. When the Zen master suddenly discovered that carrying a pail with water in it was a miracle, he realized there isn't anything except God. If you really know that, you don't need to have a religion. You can have one, because it is a free world, but you don't need one. All religion — any outward manifestation of religion — is pure gravy after that realization. It is like a man with lots of money making some more; it is quite unnecessary.

According to the very best theologians, it was never necessary for God to create the world; he did not add anything to Him. He did not have to do it, was under no compulsion. He did it out of what Dionysius the Areopagite called — to anglicize it — superfullness, or, in other words, for kicks. We do not like using that kind of language in connection with God, but it is completely contemporary and exactly right. That is what the Bible says, only it puts it in a more sedate way. It says, "His majesty did it for his pleasure." That is the way you talk about somebody who is the king. As Queen Victoria said, "We are not amused."

It says in the Book of Proverbs that the divine wisdom speaks as an attribute of God, but standing aside from God, in a sort of primitive polytheism. The goddess Wisdom says that in the beginning of the world her delight was to play before the divine presence, and especially to play with the sons of man. The word in Hebrew is "play," but in the King James translation it is "rejoice," because that is a more sedate word. You may rejoice in church, but not play. You may not have fun in church, but you may rejoice. Do you see the difference? The point of the matter is that there was no reason to make the world, and it was done just to make celestial whoopee. Alleluia. That is why the angels are laughing. Only when you hear it in church, everybody has forgotten what *alleluia* means. Alleluia is like bird's song. Birdsong is not about anything, it is just for kicks. Why do you sing? Why do you like dancing? What is music for? For kicks. That is what alleluia is. When nothing is being clung to, one gets to the point where everything blows up. That is what is meant in Zen by satori, "sudden awakening." You suddenly see, "Good heavens, what was I making all that fuss about?" Because here we are. This, right here, is what we have been looking for all the time. It was right here.

Many little children know from the beginning what life is all about, only they haven't got the words to tell us. That is the whole problem with child psychology. What child psychologists are looking for ideally is an articulate baby who can explain what it is like to be a baby, but they will never find one. By the time you teach a child to speak, you mess it up. You give it language, but it can't think big thoughts with this funny, limited language, especially using the words children are started out with. Then finally, when they've got the poor child completely hypnotized, they tell it the most preposterous things. They tell it that it must be free. They say, "You, child, are an independent agent, and you are responsible. Therefore we command you to love us. We require that you do something which will please us, and that you do it voluntarily." And no wonder people are mixed up!

I am afraid the new theology really is serious about there not being any God. The universe is therefore in rather a pitiful predicament. This is a continuation of the nineteenth century's philosophy of the fully automatic model, in which the universe is seen as essentially stupid, a mechanism, a gyration of blind energy in which human beings and human intelligence and values are flukes, and rather uncomfortable ones, because nature does not give a damn about us. And because it doesn't, we have got to fight it.

All of that is pure mythology. It is grossly unscientific, but most people believe it. It is common sense, today. But what an opportunity there is in the new theology, and in the whole ferment now going on, to get people to see another point of view, and realize that when you get rid of God, all you are doing is destroying an idol. All idols must be respectfully destroyed, but not the way those wretched Puritans went around destroying all the figures of saints in the stained glass windows in the medieval churches. That was a disrespectful iconoclasm. An example of respectful iconoclasm would be the ceremonial burning of the Bible every Easter Sunday, because if Jesus is truly risen from the dead, you do not need the Bible anymore, you do not need any books. Burn it ceremoniously, and with great respect, but not with too much seriousness, because certainly God does not take himself seriously. If He did, I should not like to think what would happen.

CHAPTER FIFTEEN

NOT WHAT SHOULD BE, BUT WHAT IS!

I WONDER WHAT IS MEANT when we use the word *I*. I have been very interested in this problem, and have come to the conclusion that what most civilized people mean by that word is a hallucination, a false sense of personal identity that is at complete variance with the facts of nature. As a result of having a false sense of identity, we act in a way that is inappropriate to our natural environment, and when that inappropriate way of action is magnified by a very powerful technology, we see a profound discord begin to separate man and nature. As is well known, we are now in the process of destroying our environment as a result of an attempt to conquer it and master it. We believe that our environment is something other than ourselves, and in assuming that, we make a great mistake and are now paying the price.

Most people would agree with the lines of the poet who said, "I, a stranger and afraid in a world I never made." We have the strong sensation that the being inside our skin is extremely different from the world outside our skin. We believe that while there may be intelligence and values and loving feelings inside human skins, outside them is a world of mechanical process that does not give a damn about any individual. We believe the physical world is a result of unintelligent gyrations of blind forces, while the biological world consists merely of gyrations of libido, Freud's word for blind lust. There are many people who say they do not believe that the world is like that, but is under the control of a wise, just, and beneficent God. Although many people say they believe that to be the case, very few in fact, actually do. A great many think that they ought to believe in God, but they actually do not, because the idea of God, as handed down in popular Christianity, Judaism, and Islam, has become implausible to most educated people. They would love to believe it, but they cannot. What was avant-garde thinking in the eighteenth and nineteenth centuries in the West — that the universe is a machine — has become the common sense of the average person of today. Most people have not caught up in their common sense with the universe of modern physics. We still think about the world in Newtonian categories, not in the categories of quantum theory.

Psychoanalysis, for example, is a Newtonian conception of our psychological mechanisms — and notice that we speak of unconscious mental mechanisms. We think of the libido in the same way as Ernst Haeckel thought of the energy of the universe as blind or unconscious. Psychoanalysis is in a sense psychohydraulics, because of its analogy between psychic energy and the flow of water. In all this, the view of the nineteenth century is that the human psyche — the mind, the ego, the superego, the id — is all basically a mechanical functioning.

The nineteenth century strove to take an objective attitude to nature and to be the very opposite of what we presume to call "primitive" animism, the point of view that sees everything as alive, held by people who converse with animals, plants, rivers, mountains, and stars. Thinkers of the nineteenth century said that this is the pathetic fallacy, a projection of intelligent human characteristics on unintelligent entities in nature. We withdrew that projection in the nineteenth century and said, "Let us look at everything objectively, as it is." Then we turned that attitude on ourselves, and studied human physiology and human psychology as objects. However, when we discovered ourselves to be objects, we decided that the time had come for suicide, because all objects, as the name implies, are of course objectionable. I found that phrase, which I thought I had invented myself, in the writings of Weston La Barre, who is a great anthropologist, but definitely of the psychoanalytic school that shares this nineteenth-century philosophy of so-called scientific naturalism. He uses the phrase "the objectionable, objective world." So when everything is deprived of subjectivity and is regarded as simply a mechanism, with nobody home as it were, then the world is seen as futile. And indeed we are preparing to destroy the planet with nuclear energy, and other processes.

I submit that this nineteenth-century view of the world is pure mythology, and not very good mythology at that. It is fundamentally based on the hallucination that we have about our own existence. It should be obvious that the human being goes with the rest of the universe, even though we say in popular speech, "I came into this world." It is not true that you came into this world. You came out of it, in the same way as a flower comes out of a plant, or a fruit comes out of a tree. An apple tree apples, the solar system — and therefore the galaxy, and therefore the whole system of galaxies in which we live — that system peoples. People, therefore, are an expression of its energy and of its nature.

If people are intelligent, and I suppose we have to grant that, then the energy that people express must also be intelligent, because one does not gather figs from thistles, or grapes from thorns. But it does not occur to ordinary, civilized people to regard themselves as expressions of the whole universe. It should be obvious that we cannot exist except in an environment of earth, air, water, and mild temperature, and that all these things go with us and are as important to us — albeit outside our skins — as our internal organs, our stomachs, and our brains.

If we cannot describe the behavior of organisms without at the same time describing the behavior of their environments, we should realize that we have a new entity of description. It is not the individual organism alone but a "field of behavior," which we must call, rather clumsily, the organism/environment. You go with your environment in the same way as your head goes with the rest of your body. However, it is not this way when we think of a person. If you suddenly think of your mother, what you think of is her face. We are used to representing people in the newspapers, magazines, books, and in art galleries with a head-and-shoulders portrait. We think of the feet, the legs, the back of the torso, as all somehow irrelevant. Here is a truncated face, and that is the person. So we say, "Put a good face on it," and endeavor to save face, to preserve the front.

Oddly enough, the very word *person* is in Latin *persona*, that through which sound passes. It refers to the megaphone mask worn by actors in Greco-Roman drama. The dramatis personae, the list of the characters to appear in the play, was originally the list of masks that were to be worn. Therefore your person, your personality, is your mask. So the question is, What is behind the mask? Notice that the whole body goes with this face. You do not find in nature faces arriving in the world sui generis; they go with a body. Also, bodies do not arrive on a plain ball of scrubbed rock floating without an atmosphere far away from a star. That world would not grow bodies. There would be no soil for bodies. There would be no body-producing complexity of environment. Bodies go with a very complicated natural environment. And if the head goes with the body, and the body goes with the environment, then the body is as much an integral part of the environment as the head is part of the body. It is deceptive, of course, because the human being is not rooted to the ground like a tree. A human being moves about, and can therefore shift from one environment to another. However, these shifts are superficial. The basic environment of the planet remains a constant, and if the human being leaves the planet, they have to take with them a canned version of the planetary environment.

We are not really aware of this relationship. On taking thought and due consideration it does occur to us that, yes, indeed, we do need that environment, but ordinarily we do not feel it. That is to say, we do not have a vivid sensation of belonging to our environment in the same way that we have a vivid sensation of being an ego inside a bag of skin, located about halfway between the ears and a little way behind the eyes. Since we feel the ego that way, and that is not the way we really exist, I call the "I" a hallucination. So, today we live with the disastrous results of the ego, which, according to nineteenth-century common sense, feels that it is a fluke in nature and that if it does not fight nature it will not be able to maintain its status as an intelligent fluke. Therefore the geneticists and many others are now saying that man must take the course of his evolution into his own hands. He can no longer trust the wiggly, random, unintelligible processes of nature to develop him any further; he must intercede with his own intelligence and through genetic alterations breed the kind of people who will be viable for future human societies. This, I submit, is a ghastly error, because human intelligence has a very serious limitation. It is a scanning system of conscious attention that is linear, and it examines the world in lines, rather as you would pass the beam of a flashlight or a spotlight across a room. The reason our education takes so long is that we have to scan miles of lines of print, and we regard that as essential information. However, the universe does not come at us in lines. Instead, it comes at us in a multidimensional continuum in which everything is happening altogether everywhere at once, and it comes at us much too quickly to be translated into lines of print or other information, however fast it may be scanned. That is our limitation, so far as the intellectual and scientific life is concerned. The computer may greatly speed up linear scanning, but it is still linear scanning.

So long as we are stuck with that linear form of wisdom, we cannot deal with more than a few variables at once. Now, what do I mean by that? A variable is any one linear process. Let us take music. When you play a Bach fugue, and there are four parts to it, you have four variables. You have four moving lines, and you can take care of that with two hands. An organist using two feet can put in two more variables and have six going. You may realize, if you have ever tried to play the organ, that it is quite difficult to make six independent motions go at once. The average person cannot do that without training. In fact, the average person cannot deal with more than three variables at once without using a pencil.

When we study physics, we are dealing with processes in which there are millions of variables. However, we handle this problem with statistics, in the same way as insurance companies use actuarial tables to predict when most people will die. However, if the average age of death is sixty-five, this average does not apply to any given individual. Any given individual will live to an individual age, and the range of individual ages at death may be very wide indeed. But that is all right, because the sixty-five guess works when you are doing large-scale gambling. In a similar way, the physicist is able to predict the behavior of nuclear wavicles. But the practical problems of human life deal with variables in the hundreds of thousands. Here statistical methods are very poor, and reaching accurate conclusions by linear means is impossible.

Now then, with such limited equipment we are proposing to interfere with our genes, and with that equipment we are trying to solve our political, economic, and social problems. Naturally, everybody has a sense of total frustration and asks, "What on earth can I do?" We do not seem to know a way of calling on our brains. This is unfortunate because our brains can handle an enormous number of variables that are not accessible to conscious attention. Your brain and your total nervous system are now handling your blood chemistry, the secretions from your glands, the behavior of millions of cells. It is doing all that without thinking about it, without translating the processes it is handling into consciously reviewed words, symbols, or numbers. When I use the word *thinking*, I mean precisely that process of translating what is going on in nature into words, symbols, or numbers. Of course, both words and numbers are kinds of symbols. Symbols bear the same relation to the real world that money bears to wealth. You cannot quench anybody's thirst with the word *water*, just as you cannot eat a dollar bill and derive nutrition from it. But scanning, using symbols and using conscious intelligence, has proved very useful to us. It has given us such technology as we have; but at the same time, it has proved too much of a good thing. We have become so fascinated with it that we confuse the world as it is with the world as it is thought about, talked about, and figured about — the world as it is described. The difference between these two is vast, and when we are not aware of ourselves except in a symbolic way, we are not related to ourselves at all, and that is why we all feel psychologically frustrated.

Thus we come back to the question of what we mean by "I." First of all, obviously we mean our symbol of ourselves. Ourselves, in this case, is the whole psychophysical organism, conscious and unconscious, plus its environment. That is your real self. In other words, your real self is the universe as centered on your organism — that is you! Now, allow me to clarify that just a little. What you do is also a doing of your environment. Your behavior is its behavior, as much as its behavior is your behavior. It is mutual. We could say it is transactional. You are not a puppet that your environment pushes around, nor is the environment a puppet that you push around. They go together, and they act together — in the same way, for example, one side of a wheel is going down as the other side of it is going up. When you turn the steering wheel of a car, are you pulling it or are you pushing it? You are doing both, aren't you? When you pull it down one side, you are pushing it up on the other. It is all one, and in the same way there is a push-pull between organism and environment.

We are only rarely aware of this in curious alterations of consciousness that we call mystical experiences or cosmic consciousness, when an individual gets the feeling that everything that is happening is of his own doing. Or it could be the opposite of that feeling, that they are not doing anything, but that all their doings, their decisions and so forth, are happenings of nature. You can feel it either way, and you can describe it in these two completely opposite ways, but you are talking about the same experience. You are talking about experiencing your own activity and the activity of nature as one single process. You can describe it as if you were omnipotent, like God, or as if it were completely deterministic and you hardly existed at all. But remember, both points of view are right, and we will see where that gets us.

We do not feel that ordinarily, do we? What we feel, instead, is an identification of ourselves with our ideas of ourselves — I would rather say, with our image of ourselves. That is the person, or the ego. You play a role; you identify with that role. I play a role called Alan Watts. And I know very well that it is a big act. I can play some other roles besides Alan Watts if necessary, but I find this one is best for making a living. But I assure you that is a mask and I do not take it seriously. The idea of my being a kind of guru, or savior of the world just breaks me up, because I know me. Besides, it is very difficult to be holy, in the ordinary sense.

So, I know I am not that, but most of us are taught to think that we are who we are called. When you are a little child and you begin to learn a role, your parents and your peers approve of your being that. In that way they know who you are. You are predictable, so you can be controlled. However, when you act out of role and you imitate some other child's behavior, everybody points the finger and says, "You are not being true to yourself. Johnny, that's not you, that's Peter." So you learn to stay Johnny, not Peter. But, of course, you are not either, because these are just images of you. They are as much of you as you can get into your conscious attention, which is precious little.

Your image of yourself contains no information about how you structure your nervous system. It contains no information about your blood chemistry. It contains almost no information about the subtle influences of society on your behavior. It also does not include the basic assumptions of your culture, which are all taken for granted and unconscious. You cannot make them conscious unless you study other cultures to see how their basic assumptions differ. Your self-image includes all kinds of illusions of which you are completely unaware, for example, that time is real and that there is such a thing as a past, which is pure conjecture. Nevertheless, all these things are unconscious in us, and they are not included in our image of ourselves, nor is there any information included in our image of ourselves about our inseparable relationships with the whole natural universe. In all this is a very impoverished image.

When you ask a person, "What did you do yesterday?" they will give you a historical account of a certain number of events in which they participated, and a certain number of things that they saw, used, or were clobbered by. You will realize at once that this history leaves out most of what happens. If I try to describe what happens to me this evening, I will never be able to describe it, because there are so many people here that if I were to talk about everyone whom I have seen, what they were wearing, what color their hair was, and what sort of expressions they had on their faces, I would have to talk until doomsday. So instead of this rich physical experience, which is very rich indeed, I have to attenuate it in memory and description and say, "I met a lot of people in Philadelphia. There were men and there were women; lots of them were young and some of them were old." Now this is an utterly impoverished account of what went on. Therefore, in thinking of ourselves in this way — in terms of this stringy, mangy account, of what I did yesterday, and the day before — all I have is a caricature of myself. Of course a caricature does not really draw us in, but just puts on certain salient features whereby people can recognize you. It's a sort of skeleton, and in this way we are conceiving of ourselves as a bunch of skeletons. They have no flesh on them, and are just a bunch of bones.

It is no wonder we all feel inadequate. We are all looking for something in the future to bring us a golden goodie at the end of the line somewhere. We hope that there is a good time coming — be it ever so far away — some far-off, divine event to which all creation moves. Therefore, when we say of something that it is no good, we mean, "It has no future." I would say, "It has no present." When everybody says, "It has no future," that is plainly ridiculous. As a result, we are psychically starved and therefore always looking, and seeking. This confused seeking is going on everywhere because we do not know what we want. Nobody really knows what they want. Instead we think of what we want in vague terms of pleasure, money, wealth, love, fulfillment, or personal development. However, we do not know what we mean by all of that.

If a person really sits down to write a twenty-page essay on their idea of heaven, it will inevitably be a sorry production. This can be seen in medieval art, where we find depictions of heaven and hell. Hell is always much better than heaven, and although it is uncomfortable, it is a sadomasochistic orgy. Hell is really rip-roaring, whereas all the saints in heaven are sitting smugly as if they were in church. Looking down you can see all the heads of the multitudes of the saved, which the artist has drawn to abbreviate them. They look like cobblestone streets.

What has happened is that our eye has been trained to see an illusion. It is merely an image, and it is no more ourselves than an idol is the Godhead. Yet we say, "That cannot be so, because I feel I really exist. It is not just an idea in my head. It is a feeling; I feel me." However, what is it that you feel when you feel "I"? I will tell you. What is the difference between looking at something and taking a hard look at it, or hearing something and listening intently? What is the difference between waiting while something goes on, and enduring it? The difference is that when you pay attention, instead of just looking, you screw up your face. You frown and stare in a futile muscular activity. When you listen intently, you start by doing some face squeezing, then you grit your teeth, or clench your fists. When you endure, you pull yourself together physically, and therefore you sit upright. You hold your breath. You do all kinds of muscular things to control the functioning of your nervous system, and none of them have the slightest effect on its proper operation. If you stare at things, you may fuzz the image rather than seeing it clearly. If you listen intently by concentrating on muscles around the ears, you will be attending to your muscles so much that you may not hear things properly. If you tighten up your body to pull yourself together, all you accomplish is to constrict yourself.

I remember sitting next to a boy in school who had great difficulty in learning to read. Teachers always say to children, "Try. If you cannot do it, you must try." So the boy tried, and when he was trying to get out words he grunted and groaned as if he were lifting weights. The teacher was impressed because the boy was really trying. The boy got a B for effort, but all he was doing was straining uselessly. We all make this muscular strain in the belief that it is achieving the sort of psychological results we intended to achieve. But this is like taking off in a jet plane, and when you get a mile down the runway and the plane is not up in the air yet, you begin to get nervous. So you start pulling at your seat belt. That is symptomatic of the chronic feeling we have in us all the time that corresponds to the word *I*.

When you see yourself as "I," you feel that chronic tension. In much the same way when an organ is working properly, you do not feel it. If you see your eye, you may have cataracts. If you hear your ears, you have ringing in your ears getting in the way of hearing. When you are fully functioning you are unaware of the body. When you are thinking clearly, your brain is not getting in your way. Of course, you are seeing your eyes in the sense that everything you see out in front of you is a condition of the optic nerves at the back of the skull. That is where you are aware of all this, but you are not aware of the eye as the eye, the optical eye. When we are aware of the ego as "I," we are aware of a chronic tension inside ourselves, and that is not us. It is just a futile tension. And then we wonder why "I" cannot do anything, why "I" feel impotent in the face of all the problems of the world, and why "I" somehow cannot manage to transform "I." Here we come to the real problem, because we are always telling each other that we should be different. However, I am not going to tell you that because I know that you cannot be different, nor can I. That may sound depressing, but I will show you that it is not. It is actually very heartening. Everybody who is at all sensitive and awake to their own problems, and humanity's problems, is trying to change themselves. We know we cannot change the world unless we change ourselves. If we are all individually selfish, we are going to be collectively selfish. As it is said in the Bible, "Thou shalt love the Lord thy God, and love your neighbor as yourself." We all agree that we must love, but we do not, and this becomes particularly appalling when we enter into the higher realm of spiritual development.

Everybody these days is interested in spiritual development, and wisely so, because we want to change our consciousness. Many people are well aware that this egocentric consciousness is a hallucination, and they presume it is the function of religion to change it. After all, that is what the Zen Buddhists, and all these yogis in the Orient are doing. They are changing their state of consciousness to get something called satori, or mystical experience, or nirvana, or *moksha*.

Everybody is really enthused about that because it is the definitive spiritual experience, and you do not get that in church. Although there have been Christian mystics, the Church has been very quiet about them. In the average church, all you get is talk —

there is no meditation and no spiritual discipline. They inter-
minably tell God what to do, as if He did not know. Then they tell
the people what to do, as if they could do what they're told, or even
wanted to. Then they sing religious nursery rhymes. And then, to
cap it all, the Roman Catholic Church — which at least had an
unintelligible service that was real mysterious and suggested vast
goings-on — went on to put the service into bad English. They
took away incense, and became essentially a bunch of Protestants,
and so now even the Catholics are at loose ends. As Clare Boothe
Luce said, "It is no longer possible to practice contemplative prayer
at mass." You are being advised, exhorted, and edified all the time,
and that becomes a bore. Think of God, listening to all those
prayers. Talk about grieving the Holy Spirit. It is just awful; people
have no consideration for God at all.

In pursuing spiritual disciplines, however, such as yoga, Zen,
and also psychotherapy, there arises a difficulty. This difficulty lies
in wanting to find a method whereby I can change my consciousness and improve myself. But the self that needs to be improved is
the one that is doing the improving, and so I am rather stuck. I find
out that the reason I think I believe in God is that I hope that somehow God will rescue me. In other words, I want to hang onto my
own existence and feel rather shaky about doing that for myself, so
I hope there is a God who will take care of it. Or I may think that if
only I could be loving, I would have a better opinion of myself. I
could face myself if I were more loving. So by some gimmickry the
unloving me has to turn itself into a loving me. This is just like trying to lift yourself off the ground with your own bootstraps; it cannot be done. That is why religion, in practice, mainly produces
hypocrisy and guilt, due to the constant failure of these enterprises.

People study Zen, and they say that getting rid of your ego is a
superhuman task. I assure you it is very, very difficult to get rid of

your ego. You have to sit for a long time, and you are going to get the sorest legs. It is hard work, and all you wretched kids who think you are getting rid of your ego with easy yoga do not know what you are in for. The biggest ego trip is getting rid of your ego, and of course the joke of it all is that your ego does not exist. There is nothing to get rid of. It is an illusion, as I have tried to explain, but still you ask how to stop the illusion. But who is asking? In the ordinary sense in which we use the word *I*, how can I stop identifying myself with the wrong me? The answer is simply that you cannot.

The Christians acknowledge this by saying that mystical experience is a gift of divine grace. Man, as such, cannot achieve this experience; it is a gift of God, and if God does not give it to you there is no way of getting it. That is solidly true, since you cannot do anything about it because you do not exist. You might say that is pretty depressing news, but the whole point is that it is not depressing news. It is the joyous news. There is a Zen poem that talks about "it," meaning the mystical experience, satori, the realization that you are, as Jesus was, the eternal energy of the universe. The poem says, "You cannot catch hold of it, nor can you get rid of it. In not being able to get it, you get it. When you speak, it is silent. When you are silent, it speaks."

This phrase — not being able to get it, you get it — is the feeling Krishnamurti tries to convey to people when he says, "Why do you ask for a method? There is no method. All methods are simply gimmicks for strengthening your ego." How do we not ask for a method? He answers, "In asking that you are still asking for a method." There is no method. If you really understand what your "I" is, you will see there is no method. We think this is so sad, but it is not. This is the gospel, the good news, because if you cannot achieve it, if you cannot transform yourself, that means that the main obstacle to mystical vision has collapsed. That obstacle was you. What happens next? By now you are at your wit's end, but what are you going to do — commit suicide? Suppose you just put that off for a little while, and wait and see what happens. You cannot control your thoughts, and you cannot control your feelings, because there is no controller. You are your thoughts and your feelings, and they are running along, running along, running along. Just sit and watch them. There they go. You are still breathing, aren't you? Still growing your hair; still seeing and hearing. Are you doing that? Is breathing something that you do? Do you see? Do you organize the operations of your eyes, and know exactly how to work those rods and cones in the retina? Do you do that? It happens, and it is a happening. Your breathing is happening. Your thinking is happening. Your feeling is happening. Your hearing, your seeing, the clouds are happening across the sky. The sky is happening blue; the sun is happening shining. There it is: all this happening.

May I introduce you? This is yourself. This is a vision of who you really are, and the way you really function. You function by happening, that is to say, by spontaneous occurrence. This is not a state of affairs that you should realize. I cannot possibly preach about it to you, because the minute you start thinking, "I should understand that," the stupid notion that "I" should bring it about arises again, when there is no "you" to bring it about. That is why I am not preaching. You can only preach to egos. All I can do is talk about what is. It amuses me to talk about what is because it is wonderful. I love it, and therefore I like to talk about it. If I get paid for it, it is because sensible people get paid for doing what they enjoy doing. My whole approach is not to convert you, not to make you over, not to improve you, but for you to discover that if you really knew the way you were, things would be sane. However, you cannot do that. You cannot make that discovery because you are in your own way so long as you think "I" am "I," so long as that hallucination blocks it. The hallucination disappears only in the realization of its own futility, when at last you see that you cannot make yourself over.

A lot of yoga teachers may try to get you to control your own mind, mainly to prove to you that you cannot do it. "A fool who persists in his folly will become wise," and so they speed up the folly. Initially you may have a certain amount of superficial success by a process commonly called self-hypnosis, and you may think you are making progress. A good teacher will let you go along that way for a while, until he really throws you by asking, "Why are you concentrating?"

Buddhism works very much in this way. Buddha said, "If you suffer, you suffer because you desire, and your desires are either unattainable or always disappointed. So cut out desire." So those disciples went away and they stamped on desire, jumped on desire, cut the throat of desire, and threw out desire. When they came back, Buddha said, "But you are still desiring not to desire." They wondered how to get rid of that desire. When you see that all of this is nonsense, there naturally comes over you a quietness. Seeing that you cannot control your mind, you realize there is no controller. What you took to be the thinker of thoughts is just one of the thoughts. What you took to be the feeler of the feelings is just one of the feelings. What you took to be the experiencer of experience is just a part of the experience.

There is not any thinker of thoughts or feeler of feelings. We get into that bind because our language has a grammatical rule that states that verbs must have subjects. The funny thing about this is that verbs are processes, and so are subjects and nouns, which are supposed to be things. How does a noun start a verb? How does a thing put a process into action? Obviously it cannot, but we always insist that there is this subject called the knower, and without a knower there cannot be knowing. However, that is just a grammatical rule, not a rule of nature. In nature there is just knowing. If you say that you are feeling, it is as if you were somehow different from the feeling. When I say, "I am feeling," what I mean is, there is feeling here. When I say, "You are feeling," I mean there is feeling there.

CHAPTER SIXTEEN

WHAT IS REALITY?

I WONDER IF IT HAS EVER OCCURRED to you how really curious it is that we regard almost everything we experience as something that happens to *us*, as something not originated by us, but as the expression of a power or an activity that is external to us. Now, if we consider the implications of this, we realize that what we mean by our *self* is narrowly circumscribed. Even events that go on inside our own bodies are put in the same category as actions that happen outside our skins. A thunderstorm or an earthquake, for instance, just happens to us — we are obviously not responsible for them. In the same way, we think that hiccups just happen to us, too, and belly rumbles just happen to us. We are not responsible for them. And as for the catastrophic fact of our being born, well, we had nothing to do with that, either. And so we can spend all our life blaming our parents for putting us in the situations in which we find ourselves.

This way of looking at the world — in a sort of passive mood — permeates our general feeling about life. As Westerners, we are accustomed to looking at human existence as a precarious event occurring within a cosmos that, on the whole, is completely unsympathetic and alien to our existence. We have been reared within an early twentieth-century form of common sense, based on the philosophy of the science of the nineteenth century, which rejected Christianity and Judaism. Therefore, we tend to regard ourselves as biological accidents in a stupid and mechanical universe that has no finer feelings and that is nothing more than a vast, pointless gyration of radioactive rocks and gas.

Alternatively — if we have a more traditional outlook — we see ourselves as children of God and, therefore, under God's authority. We believe that there is a big boss on top of the universe who has allowed us, at his pleasure, to have the disgusting effrontery to exist. So we'd better mind our Ps and Qs, because that boss is always ready to punish us, with the attitude of "this is going to hurt me more than it is going to hurt you."

When we adopt either of these worldviews — the scientific or traditional — then we are defining the world as something to which we do not really belong. We are not really part of it. I would use a stronger word than *part*, except that we do not have such a word in English. I'd have to say something like *connected with* or *essential to*.

It is quite alien to Western thought to conceive that the external world — which is defined as something that happens to us — and our bodies are *us*, because we have a myopic view of what we are. It is as if we have arbitrarily limited how much of ourselves we regard as us. It is as if we have focused our attention on certain restricted areas of the whole panorama of things that we are and have said, "I will accept only so much of me, and I will take sides against the rest."

This leads us to an extremely important principle, which can be illustrated by the fact that we see the same thing in different ways when we view it at different levels of magnification. That is to say, when we look at something with a microscope, we see it in a certain way, and when we look at the same thing with the naked eye, we see it differently, and when we look at it with a telescope, we see it in yet another way.

Which level of magnification is correct? Obviously, they are all correct. They are just different points of view. When you look at a newspaper photograph, you may see a human face. Look at that face with a magnifying glass, though, and you will see nothing but a profusion of dots, scattered meaninglessly. Move away from those dots — which seem to be separate from each other — and once again they will suddenly arrange themselves into a pattern. Those individual dots add up to something that makes sense.

Likewise, if we take a myopic view of ourselves — as most of us do — we may overlook some larger sense of us that is not apparent to us in our ordinary, myopic consciousness.

When we examine our bloodstreams under a microscope, we see that there is one hell of a fight going on. All sorts of micro-organisms are chewing each other up. And if we became overly fascinated by our view of our own bloodstream as seen in the microscope, we might start taking sides in that battle, which would be fatal to us. The health of our organism depends on the continuance of this battle. In other words, what seems like conflict at one level of magnification is actually harmony at a higher level.

Considering this, could it possibly be that we — with all our problems, conflicts, neuroses, sicknesses, political outrages, wars, and tortures — are actually in a state of harmony? Well, it is claimed that some human beings have in fact broken through to exactly that vision. Somehow or other they have slipped into a state of consciousness in which they can see the apparent disintegration and disorganization of everyday life as the completely harmonious functioning of a larger totality.

This insight depends on overcoming the illusion that space separates things. That is to say, your body and mine, our births and deaths, and the births of others after our deaths are events with intervals between them. Normally we regard those intervals in time and space as having no importance, no function. We tend to think that the universe consists primarily of stars and galaxies. They are what we notice. The space containing them is sort of written off, as if it weren't really there.

What one has to realize, though, is that space is an essential function of the things that are in it. After all, you can't have separate stars unless there is space separating them. Eliminate the space, and there will be no stars at all. And vice versa. There could be no space in any meaningful sense whatsoever if there weren't physical bodies in it. So that the bodies in space and the space surrounding them are two aspects of a single continuum. They are related in exactly the same way a back and a front are related. You just cannot have one without the other. The moment you realize that intervals in space and time are connective, you will understand that you cannot be defined exclusively as a flash of consciousness occurring between two eternal darknesses. That is the current, common-sense point of view that we Westerners have of our own lives. We consider that in the darkness that comes before our birth, we were nothing, and in the eternal darkness that will follow our death, we likewise will be nothing.

I am going to discuss these matters — not by appealing to any special, spooky knowledge, as if I've been traveling on a higher plane and remember all my previous incarnations and can therefore tell you authoritatively that you are much more than just your isolated individuality. I am going to base my discussion on common sense and facts that everybody has access to.

First of all, you have to realize that life is a pattern of immense complexity. What is the body, for instance? The body is something that is recognizable. You recognize your friends when you meet them. Although every time you see them, they are absolutely different from what they were. They are not constant, just as the flame on a candle is not constant.

We know that a candle flame is a stream of hot gas, but still we say "the flame of the candle" as if it were a constant. And we do that because the flame has a constant, recognizable pattern. The spear-shaped outline of the flame and its coloration form a constant pattern. And in exactly the same way, we are all constant patterns. And that is all we are. The only constant thing about us is our *doing* — the way we dance — rather than our being. Except that there is no *I* that dances. There is just the dancing, just as the flame is the streaming of hot gas. And just as a whirlpool in a river is a whirling of water. There is no whirlpool. There is only a thing that whirlpools. And in the same way, each one of us is a very delightfully complex undulation of the energy of the whole universe. Only by process of miseducation have we been deprived of that knowledge.

Not that there is someone to blame for this, because such miseducation is always done with our own tacit consent. Life is basically a game of hide-and-seek. Life is a pulse — on and off. Here it is, and now it isn't. And by means of this pulsation, we know life is there. Just as we know what we mean by on because we know what we mean by off. That is why, when we want to awaken someone, we knock at the door. We keep up a knocking pulsation, because that on-ness and off-ness attracts attention.

All life is this flickering on and off. And there are many different rhythms to it. There are fast flickerings, like the reaction of light upon our eyes. If we take a lighted cigarette and move it, in the dark, in a circle, we will see a circle in the air, because the image of that cigarette on our retina lasts. It endures in the same way that an image stays on a radar screen until it is revivified by another sweep of the radar antenna.

Your eye notices continuity between separate events. Very fast impulses are perceived as constant forms. We see fast impulses as solid things. When the blades of a propeller or an electric fan are turning, the separate blades become a solid disk and you cannot throw an egg through it. In the same way, you can't put your finger through a rock, even though it's mostly space. The atoms in it are moving too fast. That is the meaning of the whole phenomenon of hardness. Hardness in nature is immense energy acting in a very concentrated, restricted space, and that is why you can't push your finger through something that's hard.

Along with these very tiny and fast rhythms — which give us the impression of continuity — there are also in this universe immensely slow rhythms. And these are very difficult for us to keep track of. One very slow rhythm impresses us and depresses us as being our own life and death, our own coming and going. This rhythm moves at such a slow pace that we can't possibly believe that it is really a rhythm at all. We think of our birth as something quite unique that could never occur again. But that's only because we are so close to it, you see, and because the on-and-off pulse of our life is so slow.

From that point of view, we are, as Marshall McLuhan said, "driving a car while looking at the rearview mirror." This means that the environment in which we believe our self to exist is always a past environment. It isn't the one we are actually in.

The process of growth, which is the basic process of biology, is one in which lower orders are always being superseded by higher orders. The lower order can never — or rarely — figure out the nature of the higher order that is taking over. Therefore, the lower orders may see the higher orders as terrible threats, as total disasters, as the end of the world. We can never really know what the next step is going to be. If we did, we couldn't take it, because it would already be past. Any known future event is one of which we can say, "We've already had it." In that sense, it is past.

When we play a game such as chess, and the outcome of the game becomes certain, we stop the game and begin a new one. Because the whole zest of the thing lies in not knowing the future. The whole universe is a game of hide-and-seek. The point of that game as it is understood by the Hindus is that we don't know what the next order is going to be. But we can be sure that it will be an order of some kind, and it will comprehend us.

We are currently at a moment in history that we view as the beginning of a great countdown to the end of the human race. In this atomic age, we face the terrifying possibility that we may obliterate our planet and turn the whole globe into a cinder.

Imagine that you know exactly when the end of the world is coming. You count down to the final explosion. Seven, six, five, four, three, two, one. Suddenly there's a great roar, and you recognize it. Where have you heard it before? On the seashore, that's where, listening to the waves coming in and going out.

We don't stop to think that we are waves, too, coming in and going out. But that is what everything in the universe is. And when one wave mounts and mounts and gets too big for its boots, it spills and breaks. And we are like that. It is very important to realize that sometimes we are a crashing wave, so that then we won't panic when it happens. The person who presses the button that ends the world will be a person in a great panic. But if he realizes that waves crash and that it doesn't really matter if the whole human race blows up, then there's a chance he won't push the button. It is the only chance we have to avoid doing this thing that attracts us so powerfully, like a kind of vertigo. Or the way a person who looks over a precipice is attracted to the idea of throwing himself over. Or the way a skydiver sometimes forgets to pull the parachute ring, because he becomes hypnotized by the target — it's called target fascination. He just goes straight at it.

So, we can become absolutely fascinated with disaster and doom. That is why all the news in the newspapers is invariably bad news. There's no good news in newspapers. People wouldn't buy a newspaper consisting of good news.

Our fascination with doom might be neutralized if we would realize that every new doom is just another fluctuation in the huge, marvelous, endless chain of our own selves and our own energy.

Our problem is that, because of our myopia — because of the way we focus our consciousness upon that certain little area of experience we call voluntary action — we think that we are no more than that and that everything else just happens to us. But that is obviously absurd.

Pick up a gyroscopic top. You will notice, the minute you get it in your hand, that it has a kind of vitality to it. It seems to resist you. It starts pushing you in a certain way, just as if it were a living animal you were holding in your hand. Pick up a hamster or a guinea pig, and it always tries to escape. The gyroscope always seems to be trying to escape your hold, too.

In that same way, what you are experiencing all the time in life are all sorts of things getting out of control and doing things you don't expect. It is as if something's trying to escape your hold. But if you don't grab it too hard, you will discover that this thing that you are feeling, that feels like a gyroscope, is your own life.

You cannot understand the experience that you call voluntary action or decision or being in control or being yourself, unless there is something else in opposition to it. You couldn't realize things like self and control and will unless there were something else that is out of control — something that instead of will, won't. It is these two opposites together that produce the sensation that we call having a personal identity.

There is a funny thing about human consciousness, though, that Gestalt psychology has worked out very carefully. It is that our attention is captured by the figure rather than the background and by the relatively enclosed area rather than the diffuse area and by something that's moving rather than something that is still. To all the phenomena that attract our attention in this way, we attribute a higher degree of reality than we do to the things we don't notice.

Consciousness is a radar device that is scanning the environment to look out for trouble, just in the same way as a ship's radar is looking for rocks or other ships. And the radar therefore does not notice the vast areas of space where there are no rocks or ships. In the same way, our eyes — or rather the selective consciousness behind our eyes — pay attention only to what we think is important.

As I speak, I am aware of all of you in this room, of every single detail of your clothing, of your faces, and so on. But I am not noticing those details at all, and tomorrow I will not be able to remember exactly how each one of you looks today. What I notice is restricted to things that I think are important.

If I notice a particularly beautiful person in the audience, then that would be memorable, and I might also notice what that person is wearing. But by and large, we scan everything, but pay attention only to what our set of values tell us we ought to pay attention to. Obviously, you as a complete individual are much more than this scanning system, and you as a complete individual are in relationships with the external world that on the whole are incredibly harmonious.

Going back to the idea that the living body is like the flame of a candle, we can say that the energies of life — in the forms of temperature, light, air, food, and so on — are streaming through us all at this moment in the most magnificently harmonious way. And all of us are far more beautiful than any candle flame. Only, we are so used to our harmony and beauty that we say, "So what? Show me something interesting. Show me something new." It is a characteristic of consciousness that it ignores stimuli that are constant. When anything is constant, consciousness says, "Okay, that's safe. It's in the bag. I needn't pay attention to that anymore." And therefore we systematically eliminate from our awareness all the gorgeous things that are going on all the time, and instead we focus only on the troublesome things that might upset us.

The problem is, we make too much of it. And because we do, we identify our very self — our *I*, our ego — with the radar, the troubleshooter. And the troubleshooter is only a tiny fragment of our total being.

Now, if you become aware that you are not simply that scanning mechanism, that you are your complete organism, then you will become aware that your organism is not what you thought it was when you looked at it from the standpoint of conscious attention or from the standpoint of the ego. From the standpoint of the ego, your organism is a kind of vehicle, an automobile within which you move around. From a physical point of view, your organism is like a candle flame or a whirlpool. It is part of the continuous, patterning activity of the whole cosmos.

The key idea here is pattern.

I want to borrow a metaphor from the architect Buckminster Fuller. Imagine that we have a rope of many sections. The first section is made of Manila hemp, and the next is made of cotton, and the next is made of silk, and next is nylon, and so on. We tie an ordinary overhand knot in this rope. By putting our finger in the knot, we can move that knot all the way down the rope. As the knot travels, it's first made out of Manila hemp, then of cotton, then of silk, and then nylon, and so on. But the knot remains a knot. That's the integrity of pattern, of all patterns, including the continuing pattern that is you.

You might be a vegetarian for several years, and then you might become a meat eater. In any case, your constitution changes all the time, but still your friends recognize you, because you are still putting on the same show, you are still the same pattern. And that is what makes you a recognizable individual.

The very structure of the language we speak deceives us into misunderstanding this, however. When we see a pattern we ask, "What is it made of?" We see a table and we ask whether it is made of wood or aluminum. But when we ask what wood is made of, and how it differs from aluminum, the only answer a scientist can give is that they are two different patterns. That is to say, the molecular structures of the two are different. And a molecular structure is not a description of what something is made of, it is a description of the dance it is performing, of the symphony that it is.

All the phenomena of life are musical. Gold differs from lead in exactly the same way that a waltz differs from a mazurka. They are different dances. And there isn't any *thing* that's dancing. The belief that some thing is dancing is a deception we fall into because of our language. It has nouns and verbs in it. And verbs are supposed to describe the activities of nouns. But this is simply a convention of speech. A language could be made entirely out of verbs. You don't really need nouns. Or you could have a language made entirely of nouns, without verbs. And it would adequately describe what's going on in the world.

If you were to speak a language composed of one part of

speech, you would be able to say just as much as you can with two, and it would be a lot clearer. At first it would sound awkward, but you would soon get used to it. And when you did, it would become a matter of common sense that the patterning of the world is not the result of some thing that's patterning and that there's no substance underlying everything. There are just patterns.

Existence, for a person who really wakes up, does not consist of being a hopeless little creature confronted by a big external world that growls at it and eats it up. Every tiny little thing that comes into being, every minute fruit fly or gnat or bacterium, is an event on which this whole cosmos depends.

And that dependency goes both ways. Every little organism depends on its total environment for its existence, and the total environment depends on the existence of each and every one of those little organisms. Therefore, you could say that this universe consists of an arrangement of patterns in which every pattern is essential to the existence of the whole.

Now, we screen that idea out of our consciousness, just as we screen out the fact that space is an important reality. We pay attention to the figure and ignore the background. And so we believe that organisms are very frail and the environment is very strong. The environment lasts a long time, after all, but organisms exist for only a short time.

But what does the environment consist of? Just a lot of little things. The environment exists in just the same way that a face exists in a newspaper photograph. When you get far enough away from the tiny dots that comprise the photo, you can see the face. In the same way, when you get far enough away from all the organisms and the little bits of matter — when you change the scale of magnification — you can see the environment.

The whole environment is arranged in a system of polarities, in which the enormous depends on the tiny and the tiny depends on the enormous. There is a relationship between those extremes that can be called a transaction, similar to a financial transaction. It is impossible to have buying without selling or selling without buying. They always go together. But, of course, the person who is interested in buying tends to think more about buying than he does about selling. But if he doesn't think about the mechanisms that the other fellow is using to sell, he's going to get a bad deal. And if I want to sell something, and I think too much about selling, I won't enter sufficiently into the psychology of the buyer and I won't get the best deal for myself. I won't be a good business shark.

In this way, we always tend to overemphasize a certain aspect of our experience. In the West, there is a unique emphasis on individuality. We have made an immense psychic investment in our own individuality. We ask ourselves, What are we going to amount to? What are we going to contribute to human life? What is our particular destiny?

Individuality is a fine idea, but the thing we don't understand about it is that it won't work unless it is balanced by its opposite. Just as you can't have a back without a front, you cannot have individuality without commonality. By this I mean having another level of being at which there is no individuality at all, at which I am you and you are me.

Everyone feels that he is the center of the universe, and that everything else is happening in a circle around him. It is literally true that we can turn around and see equally far in all directions, especially if we are on a ship in the middle of the ocean. In fact, we live in a curved space-time continuum, which is a universe at which every point may be regarded as the center of the universe.

Consider a sphere. Which point on its surface is the center of its surface? You can see at once that any point can be the center. So, legitimately, each point in the universe is the center. That's St. Bonaventure's description of God: "That circle whose center is everywhere and whose circumference is nowhere." Everybody is in this situation.

At that depth of existence, we are all like the nerve ends on our own skin. At every point on our skin, there are little nerve endings gathering information from the outside world. Together, these nerve endings constitute our total sensitivity. In the same way, people, with their little eyes and ears, are all really one common center called I, which is looking at itself from ever so many different points of view.

We are so close to the center, though, and we are so absorbed in the different ways each one of us is occupying the center, that we neglect the underlying community that links us together. Individuality emerges from that community.

It's all a matter of scale.

When you get to a certain level of scale, individuality emerges from the communal background. If something with an entirely different form of biology were to come to this planet, it wouldn't know the difference between Africans, Greeks, Armenians, or Anglo-Saxons. We would all look exactly the same to it.

You can take flatworms and teach them certain tricks. If you put them in a blender, pulverize them, and feed them to untrained flatworms, the new flatworms acquire the old flatworms' tricks. Maybe one day we will take DNA from geniuses and feed it to average people and turn them into geniuses. Think of that. But the point of talking about pulverized flatworms is to show that what is transmitted is the repetition of pattern, the repetition of certain rhythms.

The great Dutch artist Escher has a book of the most fantastic patterns. One drawing may show, for example, an arrangement of devils, but when you look at the background, you see it's an arrangement of angels. In his work, everything goes with its counterpoint, so that when you look at one of his pictures you don't know what is the foreground and what is the background. You just flip, flip, flip, flip between the two, and you can see the picture either way.

Everything is like that. But we are too fascinated by whatever we, at any given moment, have selected to be the foreground to be aware of that. The foreground comes before; it is important. The background — oh, it's just background. And so, we frequently can't see the forest for the trees or the trees for the forest.

Whenever you are looking at the general panorama of sensory experience, try switching foreground and background. Try shifting your attention from all the things you think are important to all the things you think are unimportant. Look at the constants, the background. Look at the spaces *between* people, for instance.

All painters have to learn this, because they actually have to paint the background. Weavers know this, too, because when they are making patterns in weaving, they've got to weave the background as well. The people who made the great Oriental carpets were very aware that the background constitutes an essential part of the total experience of the carpet.

And so, as you become aware of backgrounds, you will notice the same thing that one notices in music: It is only as a result of hearing the interval between tones that one hears the melody. If you don't hear the interval, you will miss the rhythm and all the notes will sound like the same noise with variations of tone. To hear the melody, you've got to hear the intervals between the notes. Similarly, you've got to watch the intervals between people — the things that aren't said and the things that are implicit. And then you will begin to be connected.

It is very important to have a connection with life and to be in the know. And the fundamental way to discover that connection is to look at and see the things you usually forget or ignore. But that is the hardest thing in the world to do. And what is the most obvious thing we forget? It's the answer to the question: Who do I think I am?

How do we normally answer that question? We say our name. I'm Alan Watts. But that's not the true answer. That's only what people have told us we are. They put our names on us, and they teach us to identify with them. But we are not our names.

We know this very well. If we go back in memory to our infancy, to before people started telling us all this stuff, we will see very well who we are: the jolly old Ancient of Days. Because everybody is.

If one person realizes it and another doesn't, though, the other is a little bit offended. That's a problem. We solved it in Christianity by the very clever idea of allowing only one individual to be recognized as the Ancient of Days, as God incarnate. And since he has been safely crucified and whisked up to heaven, he can't offend us anymore. And everyone who feels an intimation of who they really are — God incarnate — and says it out loud, within Christianity, gets criticized: "Who the hell do you think you are, anyway? Jesus Christ?"

Actually, even when Jesus Christ himself said he was Jesus Christ, everybody put him down. But Christians did allow him to say who he was; they did allow that one person, that one human individual, to be the incarnation of God — but only him. In our theory of the universe, the individual is simply involved in something that is happening to him. And we feel that this thing that happens to us is reality, and that reality is something other than us. We don't recognize it as an integral part of our own being, without which we cannot know what we mean by the word *I*. But if we face the truth, every single one of us will know that there is a recess of the soul, of the psyche, where everybody understands perfectly that he is not just an irresponsible, little mouse that's been shot out into the world, but that he is really running the world.

The problem is we can't admit it, in the same way we can't admit that we are responsible for the way our own hearts beat. We say, "Oh, that's not my doing. I have no control over my heart." But do you have any control over anything? Do you have control over being conscious, for instance? Do we know how we perform an act of will? We say, "I will my hand to move from my face to my leg." We can do that, but we don't know how it is done.

Therefore, we do not understand at all what we mean by voluntary control. We might even say that the only kind of control we really understand is the kind in which we do not use our will at all. We just open and close our hand. We know how to do it, but we can't explain to someone how to do it. And we don't realize that, just as we know how to open and close our hand, we know equally well how to turn the sun into light and make the sky blue and blow the wind and wave the ocean. Just as we know how to digest food and how to be digested and transformed by bacteria. As we transform our steaks, so will we, in turn, be transformed. The patterns will continue, and the pattern is always you.

We have the marvelous capacity to transform ourselves without knowing that we are doing it and therefore to keep on surprising ourselves and therefore to keep on doing what we do. Because if we didn't surprise ourselves, we wouldn't keep on doing it. It is the very fact that we seem to be the victims of things that happen that we don't understand and that we seem to come to an end every time we die, that allows us to be alive. Every time life happens to us, it is as if it had never happened to us before. Every time we are born, it seems that we are being born for the first time. But, of course, if it didn't, we wouldn't keep on letting it happen to us.

ABOUT THE AUTHOR

ALAN WATTS WAS BORN IN ENGLAND in 1915 and received his early education at King's School, Canterbury, and the Buddhist Lodge in London, where he met Zen scholar D. T. Suzuki. He received a master's degree from Seabury-Western Theological Seminary in Illinois and an honorary doctorate of divinity from the University of Vermont.

He published his first book, *The Spirit of Zen*, at the age of twenty-one and went on to write more than twenty other books, including *The Way of Zen*, *The Wisdom of Insecurity*, and *The Book: On the Taboo against Knowing Who You Are*. In addition to being an acclaimed author and philosopher, Watts was an Episcopalian minister, a professor, a graduate-school dean, and a research fellow at Harvard University. In the early 1960s, he moved to California and began holding seminars and lectures throughout the United States. He died at his mountain retreat near Muir Woods in 1973.

NEW WORLD LIBRARY is dedicated to publishing books and other media that inspire and challenge us to improve the quality of our lives and the world.

We are a socially and environmentally aware company, and we make every attempt to embody the ideals presented in our publications. We recognize that we have an ethical responsibility to our customers, our employees, and our planet.

We serve our customers by creating the finest publications possible on personal growth, creativity, spirituality, wellness, and other areas of emerging importance. We serve our employees with generous benefits, significant profit sharing, and constant encouragement to pursue our most expansive dreams. As members of the Green Press Initiative, we print an increasing number of books with soy-based ink on 100 percent postconsumer waste recycled paper. Also, we power our offices with solar energy and contribute to nonprofit organizations working to make the world a better place for us all.

Our products are available
in bookstores everywhere.
For our catalog, please contact:

New World Library
14 Pamaron Way
Novato, California 94949

Phone: 415-884-2100 or 800-972-6657
Catalog requests: Ext. 50
Orders: Ext. 52
Fax: 415-884-2199

Email: escort@newworldlibrary.com
Website: www.newworldlibrary.com